# English Teacher Certification Exams in Texas

## Strategies for Approaching ELA/Reading TExES Exams

**Beatrice Mendez Newman**
*The University of Texas-Pan American*

PEARSON

Boston   New York   San Francisco
Mexico City   Montreal   Toronto   London   Madrid   Munich   Paris
Hong Kong   Singapore   Tokyo   Cape Town   Sydney

*To my students, for the inspiration they give me*

and

*To Donald, who makes every day a celebration*

**Senior Series Editor:** *Aurora Martínez Ramos*
**Editorial Assistant:** *Kevin Shannon*
**Senior Marketing Manager:** *Krista Groshong*
**Production Editor:** *Gregory Erb*
**Editorial Production Service:** *Walsh & Associates, Inc.*
**Manufacturing and Composition Buyer:** *Andrew Turso*
**Electronic Composition:** *Peggy Cabot*
**Cover Administrator:** *Rebecca Krzyzaniak*

For related titles and support materials, visit our online catalog at www.ablongman.com.

Between the time website information is gathered and then published, it is not unusual for some sites to have closed. Also, the transcription of URLs can result in typographical errors. The publisher would appreciate notification where these errors occur so that they may be corrected in subsequent editions.

**Library of Congress Cataloging-in-Publication Data**

Newman, Beatrice Mendez.
    English teacher certification exams in Texas : strategies for approaching ELA/Reading TExES exams / Beatrice Mendez Newman. — 1st ed.
        p. cm.
    Includes bibliographical references and index.
    ISBN 0-205-42045-1
        1. English teachers—Certification—Texas.   2. Educational tests and measurements—Texas—Study guides.   3. English teachers—Texas—Examinations—Study guides.
    I. Title.

LB1772.T4N49 2006
428'.0071—dc22

2005047620

Printed in the United States of America
10  9  8  7  6  5  4  3  2  1    HAM    10  09  08  07  06  05

# CONTENTS

Preface     vi

**1  Understanding TExES     1**

A Brief Overview     1

The TExES Framework     2

Teacher Preparation Courses and TExES     4

Study Strategies     5

Strategy 1: Learning about TEKS     5

Strategy 2: Learning from Educator Standards     8

Strategy 3: Using Test Competencies as a Study Aid     9

Strategy 4: Referencing English Course Materials     9

Strategy 5: Understanding Test Item Structure and Content     10

Strategy 6: Correlating TEKS, Standards, and Competencies     13

Organizing Your TExES Materials     14

Strategy 7: Color Coding Study Materials     14

Strategy 8: Consulting Selected Resources in Each Language Arts Area     15

Strategy 9: Keeping a TExES Journal     17

Strategy 10: Developing a Study Plan     19

Anticipating the Actual Test     20

Chapter Summary     20

**2  Reading     21**

Getting Ready to Study: Coordinating Your Reading Materials     22

A Glossary of Selected Reading Terms and Concepts     23

Classroom Practices: Reading     31

Familiarity with Grade-Appropriate Reading Materials     32

Test Item Exercises     33

Analyzing Reading Items on the Sample Test     36

Chapter Summary     36

Selected Resources: Reading Practice and Pedagogy     37

**3  Writing: Process, Practice, and Pedagogy     39**

An Overview of Writing Theory and Pedagogy     40

Coordinating TEKS, Educator Standards, and
Test Competencies in Writing     41

A Glossary of Selected Writing Terms and Concepts     41

Classroom Practices: Writing    50

Other Areas of Writing Practice and Pedagogy    51

Test Item Exercises    54

Responding to Writing Items on Sample TExES Tests    58

Chapter Summary    58

Selected Resources: Writing Practice and Pedagogy    58

## 4  Literature    61

Teaching Literature: An Overview    61

Coordinating TEKS, Educator Standards, and Test Competencies in Literature    62

A Glossary of Selected Literature Terms and Concepts    64

Classroom Practices: Literature    68

Test Item Exercises    69

Additional Study Strategies for Literature Preparation    72

Attempting the Practice Items    77

Chapter Summary    79

Selected Resources: Literature Content and Pedagogy    79

## 5  Oral Language    83

Oral Language: An Overview    83

Coordinating Oral Language Study Materials    84

A Glossary of Selected Oral Language Terms and Concepts    86

Classroom Practices: Oral Language    90

Test Item Exercises    91

Analyzing Oral Language Items on the Sample Test    94

Chapter Summary    95

Selected Resources: Oral Language    95

## 6  Media Literacy    97

An Overview of Media Literacy    98

Coordinating TEKS, Educator Standards, and Test Competencies in Media Literacy    100

A Glossary of Selected Media Literacy Terms and Concepts    101

Classroom Practices: Media Literacy    104

Test Item Exercises    105

Study Strategies for Media Literacy    108

Analyzing Media Literacy Items on the Sample Test    109

Chapter Summary    109

Selected Resources: Media Literacy    109

7   **Pedagogical Practices: Diversity,
    Technology, and Assessment    113**

      TEKS and Educator Standards    113

      A Glossary of Selected Terms in General Pedagogy    114

      A New Look at Sample Items in TExES Preparation Manuals    117

      Chapter Summary    118

      Selected Resources    118

8   **Tactics for TExES Study    121**

      Implement Your Study Plan    121

      Your TExES Journal    122

      Socialized Study: Forming a Study Group    122

      Studying the TExES Sample Items    123

      Devising Sample Units    124

    **Afterword: A Note from the Author    132**

    **References    133**

    **Index    135**

# PREFACE

If you are reading this book, you are likely taking an English language arts/reading Texas Examination of Educator Standards (TExES) soon. This test will be a significant milestone in achieving your credentials as an English language arts educator in Texas. This book is intended to help you pass your ELA TExES exam on your first try and to reduce the anxiety you probably feel about attempting this high-stakes exam.

The study strategies and information included here are aimed primarily at the two ELA content TExES exams:

- Test Field 117—English Language Arts and Reading 4-8
- Test Field 131—English Language Arts and Reading 8-12

However, there are several other TExES exams that include significant ELA components. According to the State Board for Educator Certification test bulletins (State Board for Educator Certification, 2003a-i), the following exams include ELA components that constitute from 21 to 50 percent of the total number of test items:

- Test Field 101—Generalist EC-4
- Test Field 103—Bilingual Generalist EC-4
- Test Field 104—English as a Second Language (ESL)/Generalist EC-4
- Test Field 111—Generalist 4-8
- Test Field 113—English Language Arts and Reading/Social Studies 4-8
- Test Field 119—Bilingual Generalist 4-8
- Test Field 120—English as a Second Language (ESL)/Generalist 4-8

These tests, as the test titles suggest, include sections other than ELA. This study guide will help you prepare only for the ELA components of these tests.

## How This Book Will Help You

You probably fit into one of the following teacher candidate categories:

- You are still in a teacher preparation program, enrolled in English and education courses.
- You have completed your English teacher prep courses and are planning to take an ELA or generalist TExES exam in the near future.
- You are in an alternative certification program, and you need a quick review of English test content.
- You are certified in another teaching area and are trying to become certified in English language arts or in a generalist area.

- You are an out-of-state teacher seeking certification in Texas.
- You have taken one of the TExES exams listed above but have not yet passed it.

This book will help you connect your English and education college course work to the specifications of the TExES exam you are planning to take, regardless of the route to certification you are pursuing. However, it is a *study guide*, not a comprehensive textbook, so the material presented here is highly selective and is aimed at showing you how to prepare effectively, efficiently, and pragmatically for the 4-8 and 8-12 ELA and Reading TExES exams and for the language arts components of the other exams listed above. The assumption behind this book is that you have at least some English teacher prep courses, and you need guidance in translating the vast universe of English language arts and reading content into possible TExES test item scenarios.

This book will help you regardless of the test level for which you are preparing. Anyone who has taught writing, reading, oral communication, or technology applications at multiple levels (elementary, middle school, secondary, and even college) knows that the fundamental theory, concepts, terms, and practices in these areas are the same for all levels; the difference is manifested in the level of the student audience. For example, the definitions, principles, and practices associated with a writing workshop approach are the same regardless of the grade level to which they are applied; what varies is the way the practices are adapted for a specific grade level and the way cognitive and general learning differences in students at different grade levels inform the application of writing workshop practices and principles. For the most part, the terms and practices discussed throughout the chapters apply to all teaching levels.

## What This Book Will *Not* Do

This book does not substitute for educator preparation courses; it supplements such courses by showing you how to connect state-mandated certification requirements to the content of English and reading courses. If you have gaps in your teacher preparation program (if, for example, you took no courses in writing theory and practice), this book will introduce you to terminology and ideas covered by TExES but will not provide the depth and breadth of understanding that courses in English language arts and reading would offer. Neither does this book address specialized testing areas such as English as a Second Language or bilingual education.

There are many controversial areas of ELA teaching and practice that cannot be addressed in a study guide. If you are currently enrolled in teacher preparation courses, you are likely to be discussing such topics in your classes. You should not interpret this guide's apparent lack of attention to such topics as an oversight—such discussions are beyond the scope of this book.

## Chapter Organization

Each chapter addresses a broad area of English language arts and includes the following features:

- A general introduction to the ELA area covered in the chapter.
- Test Prep Tips boxes.
- A glossary that identifies and defines key terms and concepts.
- A list of classroom practices appropriate for each ELA area.
- Test item exercises.
- Reflection opportunities that allow you to critically consider your under-standing of the knowledge and skills needed for your TExES certification level.
- Selected resources for supplemental study.

## Pragmatism and Test Preparation

A final note before we launch our test preparation: This book is *pragmatic* in nature. My goal is to provide focused, intense preparation for your TExES experience. There is no attempt to develop, change, or influence your preferences in language arts theories and pedagogical strategies. Such concerns are the domain of your teacher preparation courses and your actual teaching experience. This book will simply and straightforwardly show you how to link the content of your English and education courses to TExES content. The overriding objective of this book is to help you pass the test.

## Acknowledgments

I would like to thank the following reviewers for their time and input: Mary McDonnell Harris, University of North Texas; Angela McNulty, University of Texas at Dallas; and Susan J. Wegmann, Sam Houston University.

# 1 Understanding TExES

## A Brief Overview

TExES exams are the latest version of certification exams in the state of Texas. The conversion to TExES from the earlier certification exam, the Examination for Certification of Educators in Texas (ExCET) began in 2002. Today, teacher certification in Texas is available at three teaching levels: early childhood–grade 4 (EC-4), middle school (4-8), and high school (8-12). In addition, there are a few areas in which you can earn all-level certification. In English language arts, you can take an ELA/reading TExES at the 4-8 and 8-12 levels. There is no EC-4 language arts TExES; instead, for EC-4 and other *generalist* exams (for example, bilingual or ESL exams or the middle school generalist exam), the ELA content is only part of the total test content. Generalist exams include ELA, mathematics, social studies, science, and fine arts components. The bilingual and ESL exams include highly specialized ESL and bilingual ed content. This book addresses only the language arts components of these tests.

The English language arts content covered by TExES exams is extensive: It includes reading, writing, literature, oral language, media literacy, and other pedagogical concerns such as diversity, culture, and integration of technology. However, these general ELA areas are not given equal treatment on TExES exams. At all exam levels, the reading component is given far greater coverage than other areas (up to 50% of some generalist tests). The writing component ranks second in coverage on all exams (approximately 25%), with the literature, oral language, and media literacy constituting the remaining portion of the tests.

Regardless of where you are in your journey toward certification, it is a good idea to start planning for your TExES exam as soon as you decide to become an ELA educator. Test Prep Tip 1 is to review the state-prepared test preparation manual to get an overview of the test.

---

**TEST PREP TIP 1: READ YOUR TExES PREPARATION MANUAL**   TExES preparation manuals, available from the State Board for Educator Certification Web site (http://www.sbec.state.tx.us), offer general information about all TExES exams. Download the preparation manual relevant to your certification plans and read the sections leading up to the sample test.

---

Here's what you will find in your preparation manual: (1) a short explanation of the genesis of TExES exams; (2) the number of test items you can expect on your exam (90 for the 4-8 and 8-12 exams, 110 for the EC-4 Generalist, 190 for the Bilingual/Generalist exam); (3) a breakdown by percentage of major ELA areas covered by the exam (in other words, how much of the exam is devoted to each ELA component; (4) a list of *test competencies*, statements about the specific language arts content covered by the test (the significance of test competencies will be explained later in this chapter); (5) a sample test; (6) resources for test preparation.

Do not underestimate the importance of *reading* your TExES preparation manual. Many test candidates make the mistake of using the manual only to look at the sample test items. Without knowledge of how the test is structured, the sample items will not be useful in helping you to prepare for the test. Use the preparation manual to develop an understanding of the test *framework*.

## The TExES Framework

One of the smartest things you can do as you prepare for the TExES is to learn as much as you can about the origin, the scope, and the format of the test. Test Prep Tip 2 suggests that you visualize the test as occurring at the end of a flowchart made up of several other documents relevant to teaching in Texas.

---

### TEST PREP TIP 2: TExES FLOWCHART

**1—Texas Essential Knowledge and Skills (TEKS)**
The state's required curriculum for public school students
↓
**2—Educator Standards**
Knowledge and skills new public school teachers are expected to demonstrate;
developed by the State Board for Educator Certification
↓
**3—Competencies for Each Test**
Teacher knowledge and skills addressed by each test
↓
**4—Sample Test Items**
Included in each test preparation manual
↓
**5—The Actual TExES Exam**

---

This flowchart introduces the key terms we'll be using as we discuss TExES exams:

- Texas Essential Knowledge and Skills (TEKS)
- Educator Standards

- The Texas State Board for Educator Certification (SBEC)
- Test competencies (included in each test preparation manual)

A key objective of Chapter 1 is to help you understand the connection among these terms.

Probably the most inefficient and nonproductive strategy for "preparing" for the TExES is to take the sample test included in the preparation manuals without understanding the construction of the test or the rationale behind the test items. If you use this approach, you will literally be guessing at the answers rather than using logical, informed strategies for identifying the correct response. In fact, if you do not know how the test items are constructed, you may feel that your English and education classes have been a total waste of time. You need to understand that on the actual test, you will be faced with items that have no connection to each other. In a classroom setting, your tests have a coherence that enables you to draw on comprehensive course knowledge to respond to objective test items or to an essay exam. For example, in a course on eighteenth-century women authors, you would not find a test item that requires knowledge of how famous news photographs convey important information about social issues. But that's exactly what your actual TExES experience will be like—you will have to shift your frame of reference with each item, and that might cause you to draw a blank as you try to figure out the response.

At some point in the test preparation process, students need to learn how to maneuver through the masses of information and knowledge they acquired in their English certification courses in order to zoom in on the specific knowledge needed to successfully take an ELA TExES exam. Looking through a pair of binoculars offers a good analogy to what you have to do to prepare for the ELA TExES. When you look through binoculars trying to locate a specific image, you have to work through blurry images, figure out where all the images are in relation to each other, raise and lower your binoculars until you are in the general area that you want to focus on, and then adjust the focus to sharpen the image you want once you find it. Studying for TExES is similar to locating the image you want to see through binoculars. As a TExES candidate, you must understand from the beginning of your test preparation that the test will address only a minute fraction of the knowledge and understanding you must have to teach language arts.

Another example might help you understand the importance of the strategies presented in this chapter. Have you ever been in a class where, in the middle of a lecture or class discussion, someone asked, "Is this going to be on the test?" Teachers *hate* this question: It suggests students are only interested in passing a test and have peripheral interest in learning the course material. However, you know that having a teacher tell you what is or is not going to be on a test helps you focus your studying. With the TExES, you can't exactly ask SBEC that question. But, you can use TEKS, educator standards, and the sample test items to project the types of information that you will be tested on. If your test preparation time is limited, you want to avoid spending hours studying for material that is not likely to appear on the test. For the TExES candidate, the question "Will this be on the test?" is extremely important in structuring a study plan.

---

**TEST PREP TIP 3: WILL THIS BE ON THE TEST?**   Use TEKS, educator standards, test competencies, and sample tests as strong indicators of what might be on your TExES exam. The specificity of these documents will allow you to focus your study efforts on material that is likely to appear on the ELA/Reading TExES exams.

---

## Teacher Preparation Courses and TExES

To prepare for TExES efficiently, we need to categorize the English and reading courses you have taken in your teacher prep program in a way that will allow you to use TEKS and educator standards to study. Unfortunately, the headings used in TEKS do not correlate with the headings in educator standards, test competencies, or English program courses—a situation that could easily become confusing. So, to coordinate all of these different resources, we are going to approach our TExES preparation by identifying six major study areas: five English language arts areas and one general pedagogical practices category:

- Reading
- Writing practice and pedagogy
- Literature
- Oral language
- Media literacy
- Pedagogical practices

Chapters 2 through 7 cover these major ELA and teaching categories. Each language arts chapter includes a table that correlates applicable TEKS, educator standards, test competencies, and English courses for the language arts area addressed in the chapter.

A recurring complaint from TExES candidates is that required coursework seems to have little in common with the approach and format of the exam. At first glance, it would seem that this is a valid concern. Actually, every course in your teacher prep program can be a valuable resource for your TExES preparation; you just need guidance in figuring out how to match your coursework to the various components of the exam. This first chapter is designed to help you set up your study plan, to help you organize and correlate everything you need to draw from as you study. The ten study strategies presented in this chapter should form the basis of your study plan.

---

**A NOTE FOR EC-4, ESL, AND BILINGUAL TEST CANDIDATES:**   If you are studying for one of the generalist, ESL, or bilingual/generalist exams, this book will significantly enhance your ability to manage the *language arts components* of those tests. But, the highly specialized ESL and bilingual components are beyond the scope of this study guide.

---

# Study Strategies

## Strategy 1: Learning about TEKS

At the top of the TExES Flowchart in Test Prep Tip 2 is *Texas Essential Knowledge and Skills* (TEKS), the lengthy, grade-specific, subject-specific curriculum for Texas public school students. TEKS are based on "state-of-the-art" teaching practices; they faithfully and consistently reflect up-to-date attitudes toward language arts content and best teaching practices promoted in the most respected journals and books in the field. As public school educators in Texas, many of you will be required to identify TEKS addressed in each lesson plan you prepare—a testimony to the widespread recognition of TEKS as sound, valid, and accurate representations of learning goals for students in all disciplines and at all levels.

TExES **study strategy 1,** then, is to obtain a copy of the TEKS relevant to the TExES level you will be attempting.

---

STUDY STRATEGY 1: Download and print the English language arts Texas Essential Knowledge and Skills (TEKS) relevant to your TExES test level. You can access TEKS from the Texas Education Agency Web site (http://www.tea.state.tx.us/teks/grade).

---

To prepare *thoroughly* for TExES, you should have the TEKS for all the grades covered by the test level you are attempting. Use the list below to determine which TEKS you need:

- Test Field 101—Generalist EC-4: English Language Arts TEKS Grade K through Grade 4
- Test Field 103—Bilingual Generalist EC-4: English Language Arts TEKS Grade K through Grade 4
- Test Field 104—English as a Second Language (ESL)/Generalist EC-4: English Language Arts TEKS Grade K through Grade 4
- Test Field 111—Generalist 4-8: English Language Arts TEKS Grades 4 and 5 and Middle School English Language Arts TEKS (Grade 6 through Grade 8);
- Test Field 113—English Language Arts and Reading/Social Studies 4-8: English Language Arts TEKS, Grades 4 and 5 and Middle School English Language Arts TEKS (Grade 6 through Grade 8)
- Test Field 117—English Language Arts and Reading 4-8: English Language Arts TEKS, Grades 4 and 5 and Middle School English Language Arts TEKS (Grade 6 through Grade 8)
- Test Field 119—Bilingual Generalist 4-8: English Language Arts TEKS Grades 4 and 5 and Middle School English Language Arts TEKS (Grade 6 through Grade 8)
- Test Field 120—English as a Second Language (ESL) Generalist 4-8: English Language Arts TEKS, Grades 4 and 5 and Middle School English Language Arts TEKS (Grade 6 through Grade 8)

■ Test Field 131—ELA/Reading 8-12: English Language Arts TEKS Grade 8 and High School English Language Arts TEKS (English I [Grade 9] through English IV [Grade 12])

For test-preparation purposes, it is crucial to recognize that from the elementary through high school grade levels, TEKS are subdivided into four recurrent categories—(1) viewing/representing, (2) listening/speaking, (3) reading, and (4) writing—although they do not consistently occur in this order in every grade (Texas Education Agency, 1998a, 1998b, 1998c). Presented as knowledge and skills that *students* are expected to acquire at each grade level in each subject, TEKS statements provide the prospective TExES test taker with insights into what the state considers fundamental *teacher knowledge* in each of these categories. In other words, as you study TEKS statements that specify what students in particular grades should know about ELA, you are also learning what the state expects *teachers* to know—obviously, students can master the expected knowledge only if the teachers themselves possess that knowledge. A more compelling reason for familiarizing yourself with TEKS is the statement available on the State Board for Educator Certification (SBEC) Web site that TEKS form the foundation for educator standards (which will be addressed in the next section): "These [educator] standards are focused upon the Texas Essential Knowledge and Skills (TEKS), the required statewide public school curriculum, and they reflect current research on the developmental stages and needs of children from Early Childhood through Grade 12" (SBEC, 2004). According to this SBEC statement, then, there is a deliberate connection between TEKS and other teacher certification documents. Thus, your TExES study plan should begin with TEKS.

As a prospective test taker, you can use TEKS in several ways during your test preparation period. In many cases, relevant terms and concepts are actually defined in TEKS. For example, look at this excerpt from the reading/fluency TEKS for Grade 3:

The student is expected to:

(A) read regularly in independent-level materials (texts in which no more than approximately 1 in 20 words is difficult for the reader);

(B) read regularly in instructional-level materials that are challenging but manageable (texts in which no more than approximately 1 in 10 words is difficult for the reader; the "typical" third grader reads 80 wpm);

(C) read orally from familiar texts with fluency (accuracy, expression, appropriate phrasing, and attention to punctuation). (Texas Education Agency, 1998a)

This short passage includes explanations and definitions of three important reading terms: independent-level reading materials, instructional-level reading materials, and fluency. If you took reading courses, you are likely to have encountered these terms in your textbooks or class discussions. However, when terms such as these occur in TEKS, you should see the terms as clues about what might be on the test. Such clues occur throughout all TEKS at all grade levels. The lesson here is to recognize the ELA information embedded in TEKS. Many key terms are *simply* but—for test-taking purposes—*adequately* defined in TEKS. Collectively, TEKS will help you focus the knowledge you acquired in your teacher preparation courses. Think of the variety of topics and content you covered in your English and reading teacher preparation courses. Clearly, you cannot possibly recall everything you learned in those courses. It would be disastrous to go into a high-stakes test without knowing what aspects of your English and reading knowledge you are going to be tested on. Familiarity with TEKS eliminates a test-taking scenario in which you have no idea about what will be on the test.

Time-saving advice: If you are "down to the wire" and do not have months to prepare for your TExES, you should select *one* grade level of the TEKS applicable to your exam and study it thoroughly. For example, if you are preparing for the 4-8 TExES, you might target the Grade 6 TEKS and familiarize yourself thoroughly with the terminology and concepts presented for this grade level. If you are working toward the EC-4 TExES, you might want to target the grade 3 TEKS and make that grade the basis for your familiarity with TEKS. For the 8-12 TExES, English II (grade 10) is a good choice for your TEKS study. You can select a specific TEKS grade level to focus on as you prepare for your exam without jeopardizing your chances for success because TEKS are highly repetitious and consistent within the three certification levels. In other words, within a specific educational level, for instance EC-4, TEKS statements change very little from grade to grade. So, you can streamline your studying by focusing on a specific grade level. This is Test Prep Tip 4.

---

TEST PREP TIP 4: FOCUS ON A SPECIFIC **TEKS** GRADE LEVEL    TEKS statements change very little from grade to grade within certification levels. To streamline your studying for TExES, select a representative grade within your certification level and focus your test preparation on those TEKS statements.

---

Do not interpret Tip 4 as clearance to ignore the majority of the TEKS in your certification level. You should operationalize Test Prep Tip 4 only *after* you have read through all the TEKS grade levels applicable to your test.

As you read through TEKS, you need to keep in mind that these statements are like the "tip of the iceberg" in regard to teaching content and pedagogical principles. Underlying each TEKS statement is a wealth of *assumed* knowledge and understanding that could have been acquired only through participation in language arts and other teacher preparation courses. Reading through TEKS will put your teacher prep knowledge in the context of TExES. Ideally, as you read through TEKS, you will find yourself saying things like, "Oh, I remember discussing this in my Developing Literacy class." So, think of TEKS not as new information but as a focusing device for the knowledge you have acquired in each of the major language arts categories during your teacher preparation program.

## Strategy 2: Learning from Educator Standards

The second tier in the flowchart in Test Prep Tip 2 is *educator standards*. While the TEKS delineate what *students* should know at each grade level in each discipline, educator standards list what the *beginning teacher* at each of the certification categories (EC-4, 4-8, and 8-12) *knows and understands* and *is able to do* (State Board for Educator Certification, 2002a, 2002b, 2002c). Educator standards, produced by the Texas State Board for Educator Certification, are divided into categories roughly equivalent to TEKS subdivisions. For example, English Language Arts and Reading Standards for Grades 4-8 are subdivided into eight educator standards that cover oral language, reading, writing, media literacy, and assessment. Each standard is a broad statement about the topic addressed by the standard— for example, ELA/Reading 4-8 Standard V: Written Language: "Teachers understand that writing is a developmental process and provide instruction that helps students develop competence in written communication" (SBEC, 2002a). Each standard is further divided into two lists of descriptive statements: one list that specifies what "the beginning teacher *knows and understands*" and a second that specifies what "the beginning teacher *is able to [do]*."

Like TEKS, SBEC's educator standards offer valuable information about terms, concepts, and pedagogical strategies that might show up as test items. Thus, you can use information from educator standards as a stimulus for reviewing information suggested by the item. If the terms are unfamiliar, you can ask a professor, look in a textbook, journal article, class notes, or consult a reputable Web site for definitions.

Downloading the educator standards applicable to the TExES exam you plan to take and carefully reading and annotating those standards is **study strategy 2.**

---

**STUDY STRATEGY 2:**   Download and print the English language arts educator standards applicable to your TExES exam from the [Texas] SBEC Web site (http://www.sbec.state.tx.us).

---

You'll find the standards under the Standards and Testing heading on the SBEC Web site. There are only three sets of educator standards in English language arts, one set for EC-4, one for 4-8, and one for 8-12, and these apply even to the specialized and generalist exams.

---

**A NOTE FOR EC-4, BILINGUAL GENERALIST, ESL GENERALIST, AND 4-8 GENERALIST CANDIDATES:**   Because your tests cover multiple disciplines, you will ultimately have to study several sets of standards. For your language arts preparation, make sure you correctly download the *English Language Arts/Reading educator standards* applicable to your test and certification level. Notice that ESL and bilingual components are covered by standards specific to those areas of the test—and remember that this study guide will not address the specialized bilingual education and ESL content you need for those tests.

---

## Strategy 3: Using Test Competencies as a Study Aid

The third item on the flow chart is the *test competencies* that are included in each test preparation manual under the Test Framework heading. The competencies, like educator standards, cover broad areas of language arts: oral language, reading, literature, writing, media literacy, and diversity. Each competency is further divided into *descriptive statements* that indicate exactly what instructor knowledge each competency covers. Fortunately for test takers, there is very little difference between educator standards and test competencies. They are numbered and labeled differently, and this might cause you a bit of confusion; however, once you look at related educator standards and competencies, you will see that they cover the same information, frequently presented in virtually identical language.

  **Study strategy 3** is focused on test competencies.

---

**STUDY STRATEGY 3:** In the TExES preparation manual applicable to your TExES testing level, find the test competencies in the test framework section of the manual. Read these competencies carefully, noticing how they reiterate the information in the educator standards for your testing level.

---

  We need to take a moment to acknowledge an important aspect of the test preparation approach presented in this book: the redundancy of the materials for test preparation. Test Prep Tip 5 explains how you can use the redundancy in the various teacher certification documents to reduce your study burden.

---

**TEST PREP TIP 5: REDUNDANCY IN TEACHER CERTIFICATION DOCUMENTS** The documents devised by the Texas Education Agency (TEA) and the State Board for Educator Certification (SBEC) are actually quite redundant in content. It may seem that you are responsible for the content of numerous different state-generated documents in addition to the content of your teacher preparation courses—a situation that might make you think of TExES as an insurmountable obstacle on your journey toward certification. However, you will happily discover that TEKS, educator standards, and test competencies address the same content, TEKS from the student's perspective, educator standards from the beginning teacher's point of view, and test competencies in the context of actual test items.

---

Refer to Test Prep Tip 5 if your test preparation resolve grows shaky. This tip should keep you from making a rash decision to forego examining the documents produced by TEA and SBEC. Being familiar with TEKS, educator standards, and test competencies is not an option in your TExES preparation—it is the beginning point of your TExES study.

## Strategy 4: Referencing English Course Materials

An important part of your preparation for TExES is assembling books, articles, essays, projects, tests, and notes from your English and education courses. This is

**study strategy 4.** The knowledge you acquire in such courses is the foundation that will support you as you move forward in your test preparation. Even if your professors never mentioned TExES in their class discussions and lectures, the material they presented in class is vital to your TExES readiness. As we go through each major language arts area in the chapters that follow, you should have your course materials readily accessible. You probably will not have time to review those in depth, but you can use them to clarify and amplify information that will be presented in the chapters that follow or in the TEKS, educator standards, and sample items from your TExES preparation manual.

---

**STUDY STRATEGY 4:**  Locate and organize course materials that you can use as references during your TExES study periods.

---

Each chapter that follows includes a study chart that shows what types of courses are applicable to each language arts category covered in your TExES exam. For now, you should try to assemble the following materials from your advanced English, communication, reading, and literacy courses:

- Textbooks
- Major projects, particularly teaching-related projects, that you may have completed in these courses
- Class notes
- Supplementary texts, handouts, and articles
- Tests and essays

## Strategy 5: Understanding Test Item Structure and Content

The fourth item in the TExES flowchart is the sample test. Notice that the test items—sample and actual test items—are positioned at the *end* of the flowchart. While you might be tempted to begin your test preparation by looking at sample test items, you need to understand that effective test preparation has to encompass the other elements in the flowchart. **Study strategy 5** is to learn how TExES objective items are constructed so that you can use your knowledge of English language arts, of TEKS, and of educator standards to "figure out" the correct response.

---

**STUDY STRATEGY 5:**  Learn about the construction of TExES objective items.

---

To respond successfully to the actual test items, you should possess some knowledge about the format of TExES items.

■ TExES sample and actual test items fall into two categories: (1) *content* items that test knowledge of fundamental terms and concepts in language arts areas and (2) *pedagogy* items that test your ability to apply best teaching practices in hypothetical classroom situations (what we commonly call "teaching scenarios"). Content items are you-know-it-or-you-don't types of items; analyzing the language of the item and the responses will not help you figure out the correct answer, whereas it is possible to intelligently "guess" the correct response to pedagogy items by carefully analyzing the item prompt or stem and the response options.

■ Each item is made up of a stem and a list of four possible responses. In a well-constructed objective item—the type you will encounter on your TExES exam—the stem directs the test taker to focus on the specific knowledge that the item is designed to test. A savvy test taker knows that the stem provides valuable clues that can be used to eliminate inappropriate responses and to confidently select the response that corresponds to the focus overtly or implicitly presented in the stem. As soon as you start reading the item stem, you should identify the item as a reading, writing, literature, oral language, or media literacy item.

■ Objective items on the TExES may be single or clustered items. If an item is part of a "cluster," this means that several objective items are based on a scenario or text or situation presented at the outset of the multi-item cluster.

■ Well-constructed objective items do not include "trick" responses. The objective of items such as those produced by National Evaluation Systems, Inc., the organization that produces TExES, is to give the test taker opportunities to demonstrate his or her mastery of the material being tested. If you walk into the test environment knowing how the test is constructed, you will never have the sense that the test maker is "out to get you" with trick questions—and this knowledge should boost your confidence in your ability to achieve a passing score.

■ TExES item stems and responses may be "deconstructed" by recognizing TEKS, educator standards, test competencies, and/or teacher prep course content reflected in the stem and the four responses.

■ There is no superfluous language in test item stems or responses. You need to read each item and each response with the awareness that *every word counts.*

■ TExES test items and related competencies and standards—regardless of whether test constructors and state agencies admit this—represent *ideal* classroom situations. It is important to remember, as you analyze responses to test items on the sample test, that regardless of whether you might consider a specific response an interesting, effective classroom activity, you must stay focused on the teaching practices and ELA content specified in TEKS, educator standards, and test competencies. In other words, you should avoid picking a response simply because it describes a fun activity, because it seems to encourage students' creativity, or, if you are already in a classroom, because it is an activity you have used successfully. You must focus, instead, on the extent to which the response you choose reflects the attitudes and approaches conveyed in TEKS and educator standards and the degree to which the response corresponds to the specifications of the item stem.

■ For many objective items, all the responses appear to be correct; that is, they may all reflect sound teaching practices. The key to identifying the correct response, as we will see in the analyses of practice test items, is to stay focused on the qualifying language of the stem. The stem may include words such as *first, best, initial, only* that help you eliminate inappropriate responses. All the stems will also include language that focuses the item on a specific type of language arts goal or activity.

Use Test Prep Tip 6 to keep focused on the language of the item stem as you tackle the sample test items and as you eventually face the actual test items.

---

### TEST PREP TIP 6: UNDERSTANDING THE STRUCTURE OF TEST ITEMS

1. Notice the stem structure: Is it a content or pedagogy item? If it's a pedagogy item, take note of the teaching scenario described because it will help you establish parameters for the scope of the item. Also note the instructional goal or student outcome included in the stem.
2. Determine what area of language arts the item addresses. In almost every item, there will be enough clues to help you categorize the item as a reading item, a literature item, a media literacy item, an oral language item, a writing item, or a general pedagogy item.
3. Use your knowledge of TEKS and educator standards (Study Strategies 1 and 2) to identify key terms in the stem and focus your attention on those terms as you work at identifying the correct response.
4. Circle or underline important terms in the stem that further qualify each test item, e.g., *initial, beginning, next, additional, assessment, students with learning difficulties.*
5. Remind yourself of definitions or teaching practices related to key terms in each item stem.
6. Pay close attention to the question that ends the stem; in most cases, it further limits the possibilities for the correct response.
7. As you read each possible response, ask yourself, "To what extent does this response fit the limitations established by the stem?"
8. Eliminate responses that violate the limitations established by the stem.
9. In pedagogy items, be aware that all the responses are likely to sound correct. Keep in mind that eliminating a particular response does not mean that the activity described in the response is unsound: It merely means that the activity does not meet the specifications of the stem.
10. Do not select the correct response until you have evaluated all of the responses and are satisfied that your choice best meets the specifications of the item stem.

---

A few words of warning to those of you who are already functioning in classrooms as student teachers, alternative or accelerated certification interns, emergency certificate holders, or teachers certified in other states: What you do in your classroom for pragmatic reasons may not always reflect the spirit and content of TEKS, educator standards, or test competencies. All of us do things in our classrooms that are triggered by immediate, idiosyncratic, and spontaneous situations. The fact that you have actually used some of the activities mentioned in item responses should not be an indication that a particular activity represents the right response to the item. In fact, for most items, all four responses will seem "good" responses because all the responses represent activities that work well in the classroom. As you prepare for TExES, you need to discipline yourself so that you don't let yourself be swayed by a response that sounds like a "cool" class activity. Instead, use the steps in Test Prep Tip 6 to discipline yourself to select the right response.

The sample tests in each preparation manual are useful for helping you estimate how much effort you need to expend in studying for various areas of the test, particularly as you contrast the areas in which you feel strong and those for which you might feel inadequately prepared. The bottom line—as you examine the sample test items—is that you may not have covered large chunks of the test material in your teacher prep courses. Topics like media literacy, student diversity, assessment, and the structure and development of English may have been covered peripherally in your coursework—or you may not remember studying the information. Furthermore, the content that you were expected to master in your language arts courses may not be the same as the information included in TEKS, educator standards, and test competencies. If you are an English major, you can probably breeze through items related to analysis and interpretation of literature and items related to the writing process, but unless you took methods courses in literature and writing, you may not be able to pick out correct responses to items that cover teaching practices in literature and the writing process.

The sample tests, then, serve primarily to give you an idea of the type of questions you will face on the actual test. The items themselves are not very helpful in terms of reviewing or preparing. What you need, instead, is focused knowledge and test-taking strategies—which you will find throughout this book.

## Strategy 6: Correlating TEKS, Standards, and Competencies

If by this point, you are confused about TEKS, educator standards, and test competencies, don't be distressed. It can be confusing! The good news is that despite the different labels, their content is redundant. The "trick" is to coordinate related TEKS, standards, and competencies and to study these in juxtaposition to each other (as opposed to reading through all the TEKS, then all the standards, and then all the competencies). The repetitive nature of TEKS, educator standards, and test competencies should indicate the efficacy of studying these documents in conjunction with each other. Let's say you are studying for the oral language component of the 4-8 ELA/Reading TExES. By the time you read through all the listening/speaking TEKS for grades 4-8, through the descriptive statements for the oral language educator standards, and through the oral language test competencies for middle school, you will have a very good idea of what terms, concepts, and teaching skills are included in the oral language component of TExES. Each chapter that follows will include a chart to show you how to coordinate specific TEKS categories with relevant educator standards and competencies for each language arts area that your TExES level covers.

Study strategy 6 is to correlate TEKS, educator standards, test competencies, and your course materials in each language arts area covered by TExES.

---

**STUDY STRATEGY 6:**   Correlate all materials (TEKS, educator standards, test competencies, and course materials) relevant to each language arts area as you study.

---

## Organizing Your TExES Materials

Before you move much further into your TExES preparations, it would be a good idea to assemble the various documents we'll be using into an organized three-ring binder with dividers. I suggest you use a 2 1/2-inch, three-ring binder since you'll be adding materials throughout your TExES study time. Put the TEKS relevant to your TExES exam in section 1, the educator standards for your test level in section 2, and the TExES Preparation Manual in section 3. Reserve several sections for articles and other materials you add as you read through this book. Studying for TExES can turn into a messy, confusing process—you'll have all sorts of documents that you've downloaded from the SBEC and TEA Web sites, and you need to keep them organized and available as you proceed through your study plan.

Studying from computer files of these documents may seem efficient to you since you won't have to keep track of paper copies, but this actually is not a very productive study strategy. Studying from hard copies of the TExES materials will allow you to annotate the various documents, to cross-reference them, to jot down questions to yourself, to highlight key terms. The next strategy—color coding each language arts area—will increase your efficiency in studying.

### Strategy 7: Color Coding Study Materials

As you prepare for your exam, you will be handling at least three separate documents: TEKS, educator standards, and the preparation manual. In addition, you will have books and other materials from your teacher prep courses (study strategy 6). It will be very easy to become confused and to spend a lot of time leafing through pages and pages of documents trying to find sections related to specific language arts areas. So, I suggest that you color code your study materials by designating a color for each major English language arts area and marking TEKS, educator standards, test competencies, and sample test items for that area in a dedicated color. For example, you can highlight and/or mark everything related to writing theory and pedagogy in light blue, everything related to media literacy in pink, etc. and flag these areas with adhesive flags in matching colors so that you can locate each language arts area quickly.

Color coding, **study strategy 7,** will enable you to visually coordinate the various components of your study material. If you are studying seriously and regularly, you will have materials scattered all over your study area, and the color coding will save you time and effort and cut down on confusion. For example, if you have flagged and highlighted each language arts category and you are studying media literacy on a particular afternoon, you can go directly to the color you have designated for media literacy (instead of leafing through pages and pages of TEKS and educator standards).

---

STUDY STRATEGY 7:   Color code TEKS, educator standards, and test competencies according to language arts areas to make your studying more efficient.

---

Each chapter in this book will suggest a color code for that language arts area, but you can choose your favorite colors. I suggest you acquire pens, highlighters, and flags in yellow, blue, orange, green, pink, purple, and whatever other colors you can find in your office supply store.

## Strategy 8: Consulting Selected Resources in Each Language Arts Area

Each chapter, beginning with this one, includes suggested readings designed to enhance your understanding of language arts. These resource lists are *selective* and *representative* rather than *definitive*. There is no claim here that the suggested resources are the best or only resources. Neither should you consider the suggested books and articles as substitutes for a formal teacher education program.

The resources are of two basic types: books that focus on teaching language arts and articles that illustrate teaching applications of language arts approaches. The books, in addition to excellently explaining language arts concepts and teaching practices, have indexes that you can use to locate specific terms and definitions in a hurry. The articles, primarily from journals of the National Council of Teachers of English (NCTE), have been selected on the basis of how they illustrate classroom practices that reflect the pedagogical approaches and teaching activities suggested by TEKS, educator standards, and test competencies. Since we are dealing with three testing levels, the annotations indicate whether the resources are most applicable to EC-4, 4-8, or 8-12 preparation. In most cases, however, the resources provide useful information for all testing levels.

**Study strategy 8** advises you to consult some of the resources included at the end of each chapter in order to enhance your understanding of the material you will be tested over.

---

**STUDY STRATEGY 8:**    Consult suggested resources in each language arts area.

---

***Comprehensive Resources.***    Each of the books listed here as comprehensive resources includes general coverage of the language arts areas addressed in TExES examinations. These books are helpful primarily because of their discussion of the terms and concepts you will encounter in TEKS and educator standards. If your teacher preparation program has not included one of these books or similar books as required course materials, you should read the annotations and select at least one of these comprehensive ELA pedagogy textbooks to include in your study plan.

Burke, J. (2003). *The English teacher's companion* (2nd ed.). Portsmouth, NH: Heinemann.
> Written by a long-time ELA teacher, this book seems to cover every teaching concern and teaching situation secondary level ELA teachers may face. If I were a new English language arts teacher, Burke's book would be my bible. Burke draws on an impressive bank of knowledge to offer the new teacher activities, strategies, handouts, and units that can be implemented "as is" and provides actual samples of student responses to activities described in the book. The TExES candidate will learn definitions of important ELA terms and will understand how ELA strategies can be implemented in classrooms. There are chapters on reading, on vocabulary, on grammar, on writing, on oral language, on critical thinking, on assessment, and on media literacy. There is no separate chapter on teaching literature, but information about that area is integrated into the reading chapter.

Christenbury, L. (2000). *Making the journey: Being and becoming a teacher of English language arts* (2nd ed.). Portsmouth, NH: Heinemann.
> Christenbury's reflections on what works in the classroom are based on theory and her vast experience as a middle school and high school language arts educator. This book includes chapters on teaching literature, language, writing, questioning (oral language), and media literacy. Although no chapter on reading is included, chapter subheadings indicate that some areas of reading instruction are covered. Another valuable chapter for the TExES candidate is the chapter on students, which can be used to develop an understanding of diversity in the classroom. The detailed table of contents includes terms and headings that could have been taken from TExES-related materials; thus, the TExES candidate will find this book a valuable resource in making sense of the terminology in TEKS and educator standards.

Bertrand, N. P., & Stice, C. F. (2002). *Good teaching: An integrated approach to language, literacy, and learning.* Portsmouth, NH: Heinemann.
> This is a book that EC-4 TExES candidates should read if they have months instead of weeks to prepare for the test: This book should not be read quickly or superficially but should instead be read with a great deal of consideration. Bertrand and Stice explain the theories behind elementary level classroom practices, and their title is right on target: It is almost impossible to separate aspects of ELA in their discussion. This book includes much more detailed and elaborate definitions of ELA terms than do most of the other comprehensive books cited here. Many of the terms and concepts that occur in TEKS and educator standards are explained thoroughly in this book.

Maxwell, R. J., & Meiser, M. J. (2005). *Teaching English in middle and secondary schools* (4th ed.) Upper Saddle River, NJ: Prentice-Hall.
> This book offers an excellent combination of theory and practice in major areas of language arts pedagogy: diversity, integrating ELA, oral language, writing, literature, grammar, language, assessment, thematic units. Though it lacks attention to reading and to media literacy, many other features make this a valuable TExES prep resource. Each chapter integrates

theory with practical concerns and includes numerous teaching activities and instructional units. For the TExES candidate doing last-minute preparation, it would be a good idea to examine several of the complete instructional units included in the book to get a sense of how pedagogical principles can be transformed into actual classroom activities.

McGee, L. M., & Richgels, D. J. (2004). *Literacy's beginnings: Supporting young readers and writers* (4th ed.). Boston: Pearson Education.

The EC-4 TExES candidate will find this book a "must have" resource. The book is organized by learning levels (child's age) rather than language arts areas. Key terms are boldfaced, chapters are divided into usefully labeled subdivisions (which makes it easy to find sections on particular TExES-relevant topics), and plentiful examples of children's writing and language arts performances are integrated throughout the book. The list of key concepts at the beginning of each chapter and the nicely subdivided and subtitled chapter sections make it possible for the TExES candidate to use this book to quickly find definitions and explanations of terms encountered in TEKS and educator standards.

## Strategy 9: Keeping a TExES Journal

When I conduct study sessions for TExES exams, I am always approached by students who have been taking notes while studying for the exam, usually on legal pads or in the margins of their TExES Preparation Manual. These students have questions about particular terms, specific test sample test items, and issues they have thought about during their independent study sessions. Even if you are studying at the last minute (your test is only a few weeks away), you should reflect about what and how you are studying. I suggest you keep a TExES journal. I probably have hundreds of documents (e.g., articles, study session handouts, exercises) and possibly several hundred books I use in working with my certification candidates. However, I have a 6 1/2 × 9 1/2-inch dark green spiral notebook in which I keep notes to myself and ideas for working more effectively with TExES candidates. I would be lost without my notebook; I check to make sure it is in my book bag before I go to work each day, and when I travel, it is one of the first things I pack in my carry-on satchel. Figure 1.1 shows a page from my TExES journal.

Like many authors, I use journal entries such as this one to remind myself of what I need to address in my book. Although I compose at my computer, I think of ideas throughout the day when I am not directly working on my writing projects. This particular entry shows notes I took as I studied EC-4 TEKS for writing, but my journal is filled with similar notes about terms, reminders to include explanations of certain terms that I may have overlooked in earlier drafts, references to books, ideas for composing sample items, outlines for paragraphs or sections to include in chapters, and my own observations about language arts practices.

Keeping a journal in which you reflect about your studies, your concerns, your anxieties, and your understanding about English language arts is a good strategy for optimizing your study activities. (And it is a strategy you want to pass on to your own students.) In your journal, you can enter notes to yourself about terms to explore in greater depth than what is provided in this book; you can jot down questions to ask a professor or the certification coordinator in your discipline; you can make connections between things you've done in your

---

*8-2-03*

*WRITING CHAPTER—EC-4 Content*

*journal writing*

*transitional spelling      invented*

*phonetic spelling————orede——>all ready*

*invented spelling—point out even older writers invent spelling! caious*

*author's chair——>journal entries*

*spelling logs*

*blends*

*orthography*

*orthographic patterns—spelling rules that children gradually learn . . . reflected in writ-
ing . . . . –res, -es/s, —doubling consonants*

*word boundaries (concept of word boundaries)*

*conventions—EC-4—capitalization—punctuation (end punc.)—mechanics (apostro-
phes/hyphens)*

*left-to-right organization—top-to-bottom*

*audience awareness— TEKS as early as Grade 1*

*"forms" of writing— Term used in TEKS to distinguish among purpose/audience gener-
ated texts such as lists, letters, stories*

*For EC-4 question: Use passage from Meanwhile Back at the Ranch first grade sum-
maries——>teacher's assessment of students' writing competence*

*\*\*\*\*\*Writing chapter—teaching writing to young children incorporates initial under-
standing about what constitutes writing (not necessary with older students)*

---

**FIGURE 1.1   Sample TExES Journal Page**

English and education courses and what you are reading in the TEKS and educator standards applicable to your test. Reflection is a good way to involve yourself
completely in your TExES study process. So, **study strategy 9** is the suggestion
that you keep a journal during your study process. Get yourself a small spiral
notebook that you carry with you all the time; or, if you are a palm pilot or computer notebook type of person, create an electronic folder for your TExES reflections, questions, and notes.

Each chapter will include several prompts for you to enter reflections in your TExES journal.

## Strategy 10: Developing a Study Plan

Once you get serious about taking your designated ELA/reading TExES (in other words, once you have a test date in mind), you should devise a plan of study to help you make the best use of the time you have available for studying. Here are some suggestions for developing your study plan:

■ Work in study time each day, even if it is only 30 minutes. Ideally, you should try to study at the same time every day. Think of this study plan the way joggers think of their jogging time: Most serious joggers carve out their jogging time out of all other required daily activities, sometimes choosing jogging over other daily activities. While you do not have to be fanatic about your TExES study, you do need to be disciplined and dedicated.

■ Study by the language arts categories covered in each chapter: Study everything related to writing in one chunk, everything related to literature, etc. Remember to use the study charts included in each chapter to organize all materials related to each language arts category.

■ You should actually chart out your study plans on a calendar so that you devote adequate time to each area of TExES and so that you stay on a schedule. Otherwise, you may end up allowing yourself to skip so many study periods that by the time you get back to your study plan, you are likely to have forgotten important basic information and will have to spend time relearning it. Back to the jogging analogy: One reason that serious joggers push themselves to jog even when they don't feel like it is that it is very difficult to build up the stamina and conditioning lost when the running schedule is abandoned. And, just as a jogger can't prepare for a marathon by running a couple of miles every once in a while, neither can a TExES candidate adequately prepare for the exam by cramming for it a day or so before the test date.

■ Make sure you use TEKS, educator standards, test competencies, and the sample test items in the ways suggested in the chapters in this book.

## Anticipating the Actual Test

The last item in the TExES flowchart is the actual test. Test Prep Tip 7 offers some final test-taking advice.

---

TEST PREP TIP 7: FINAL PREPARATIONS

1. Start studying as soon as you decide when you will be taking the test, even if you haven't registered for it yet.
2. Stick to your study plan.
3. Try to carry some sort of test prep materials with you everywhere you go once you start studying in earnest. If you are stuck waiting somewhere, you can use your waiting time to study.
4. Vary the way you study: Sometimes study at your desk; sometimes read poetry and fiction in a comfortable environment; study in the car if you are a passenger; organize study groups with fellow test takers.
5. Try to read at least some of the resource materials suggested in each chapter.
6. Do not limit your test preparation to "cramming" for the test in the last two days before your exam. It is very possible that there are many certification candidates who can adequately prepare for the test in this way, but it is a far wiser to spread the preparation over the six weeks or so between your registration date and the actual test date.
7. If you are still enrolled in teacher preparation courses, ask your teachers to show you how the course content is related to TExES content.

---

The study strategies presented in this chapter are intended to give you an edge as you prepare for the test and to give you a general idea of the scope of the preparation required. Chapter 8 discusses more extensive, focused *tactics* for test preparation that you can implement after you understand the content of the test, in other words, after you have worked through Chapters 2 through 7.

## Chapter Summary

- To study effectively for your TExES exam, download and print TEKS, educator standards, and the test preparation manual from the TEA and SBEC Web sites. Do not think of this as an optional strategy—these documents are vital to your preparation.
- Organize your TExES documents in a three-ring binder.
- Apply the 10 study strategies presented in this chapter.
- Locate materials from your teacher prep courses (books, notes, etc.) and use these as reference materials as you study.
- Devise a study plan that includes regular study sessions from the time you decide to take the TExES until the day you are scheduled to take the exam.

---

REFLECTION FOR YOUR TExES JOURNAL:   How prepared do you believe you are for your TExES exam? Are you anxious about taking it? What is the source of the anxiety? How do you intend to prepare for the exam?

---

# CHAPTER

# 2  Reading

"Reading" is the general label used to refer to structured classroom instruction and practices that promote literacy. If you have had no formal training in teaching reading, you need to recognize that the reading components of TExES exams are not intended to test your competence in the *process* of reading but your competence in *teaching* reading. Reading instruction encompasses a vast array of topics such as phonics, vocabulary development, word recognition skills, comprehension, fluency, oral reading, and reading rate. Reading is so vast an ELA subject area that it would be reductive to try to define it succinctly, but as you proceed through your TExES study plan—particularly if you lack comprehensive ELA preparation—you should have a *working* definition of reading. Focus on the "working" aspect of the definition: This definition is aimed at helping you differentiate *reading* from other language arts areas rather than at providing a definitive, absolute explanation of reading as an activity or teaching field.

---

READING: A WORKING DEFINITION    Reading is a language process that involves construction of the meaning conveyed through a written text. A reader must rely on a vast array of language competencies—phonetic knowledge, word recognition skills, vocabulary, syntax, prior knowledge, metacognitive skills, and many, many others—to read fluently and proficiently. Reading is a developmental process that continues throughout the learner's experiences in classroom and other learning environments (which include the home setting). In the classroom setting, reading is a social as well as individual activity. Classroom approaches to literacy instruction should include fostering in students a lifelong love of reading.

---

For the most part, intensive reading instruction is focused on young children, and substantive amounts of classroom time are devoted to developing all aspects of the young learner's literacy. However, structured reading instruction continues through middle school, and in high school, it is integrated into other language arts areas. You should also note that reading instruction at the high school level is not exclusively the domain of the developmental or support staff. In other words, we do not teach reading in high school to help students reach appropriate reading grade levels; we teach reading in high school because students are still learning the language of particular academic fields, because they need to continue to expand their vocabulary, and because they need reading strategies to help them tackle increasingly complex texts. All levels of TEKS and educator standards include substantive reading components, so you should be prepared to respond to numerous questions in these areas on the reading component of the ELA TExES you take.

If you have had no courses in reading in your teacher prep program, it would be a good idea to read one of the books listed in the Selected Resources section in this chapter. Reading is a specialized, complex discipline. The material in this chapter only begins to touch on key concepts and terms in reading. Under no circumstances should you think of this chapter as a substitute for formal instruction in reading theory and pedagogy. Keep in mind that this chapter is aimed at helping you identify key terms that you can pull out from TEKS and educator standards to predict what might show up on your actual TExES exam.

Before you start your organized study of the reading component, take some time to reflect on your own literacy acquisition, on your attitude toward reading, and on your reading practices.

---

REFLECTION FOR YOUR TEXES JOURNAL:   What do you remember about learning to read? Where does reading rank in the hierarchy of activities that matter to you? How do you work through difficult texts? What do you like most about reading?

---

## Getting Ready to Study: Coordinating Reading Materials

To begin your study sessions in the area of reading, you need to coordinate sections from the documents on which the test items are based. Let's designate yellow as our color coding for reading (Study Strategy 7). Before you proceed with this chapter, highlight or flag in yellow the following sections of your study documents:

- TEKS: All *reading* categories excluding those that are subdivided into literary response and literary concepts. (These literature-related TEKS will be addressed in Chapter 4: Literature.)
- Educator standards and test competencies: All standards that address phonetic and/or alphabetic principles, comprehension, fluency, vocabulary development, word identification, research, and literacy.
- Sample test items: All items related to reading test competencies. Each sample test item has the relevant competency printed at the bottom of the page.

The chart in Figure 2.1 will help you organize your TEA and SBEC materials for efficient studying.

You should read the TEKS items, the educator standards, and the test competencies carefully and studiously to familiarize yourself with the terminology and ideas related to teaching reading. Before you proceed through the rest of this chapter, you should reflect on your general understanding of the material covered by TEKS, educator standards, and test competencies related to reading.

---

**REFLECTION FOR YOUR TExES JOURNAL:**   As you read through the TEKS categories, the educator standards, and the test competencies related to reading, make a list of terms you are not sure about, jot down questions that occur to you, and annotate your materials with notes that link the SBEC and TEA documents to your reading coursework. Try to remember activities you did in your courses that reflect the content of these documents. This reflection will activate your prior knowledge of the terms presented in the glossary and of the teaching practices explained later in this chapter.

---

## A Glossary of Selected Reading Terms and Concepts

The terms defined and/or explained below have been compiled mostly from TEKS, educator standards, and test competencies relevant to literacy development and reading comprehension. The explanations provided in the glossary below are minimal—to fully understand any term unfamiliar to you, you must look it up and read about it more extensively in a reading textbook or one of the articles annotated in the Selected Resources section of this chapter. If you have taken reading or literacy courses, you should refresh your understanding of the terms by referring to textbooks and notes. Terms and concepts related to *literature*, although embedded in reading TEKS, will be covered in Chapter 4.

**alphabetic principle:**   The concept that the symbols of the English alphabet represent sounds. This is an important concept for *emergent readers* to grasp before they can move to higher levels of reading proficiency. It is essential that emergent readers understand that alphabet symbols are arbitrarily paired with the sounds they represent—for example, that there is nothing about the letter A, or any other letter, that links it to the sounds it represents.

**basal readers:**   Books that are part of a systematic, skills-based reading program in which students move through progressively more challenging texts as their reading skills improve. Basal reader programs include a variety of teaching materials (such as vocabulary activities, response activities, workbook exercises, etc.) designed by the basal reader publisher rather than developed by the classroom teacher in response to specific learner needs. Basal reader programs are sometimes referred to as "published school reading programs."

**challenging text:**   A text that includes vocabulary, concepts, terms, syntactic structures, and other elements that are beyond the reader's current independent reading level. A challenging text may be selected by the teacher to encourage the reader to use metacognitive skills to move to a higher level of comprehension. However, if a text is too challenging, the reader may feel frustrated and will be unable to adequately demonstrate comprehension skills.

**choral reading:**   An oral reading and/or oral language activity in which students orally read in unison a short section of a text. In a common application, students function as a chorus by uttering in unison a line that is repeated almost as a refrain throughout a text. This activity develops oral listening skills as well as literacy skills: By paying attention to the progression of the story and by anticipating the point at which the repeated line occurs, students learn about text structures and rhetorical strategies. In addition, this is a highly social activity that helps students appreciate reading as an entertaining language activity.

FIGURE 2.1  Reading Study Chart

## EC-4

| TEKS K-4 | Educator Standards | Test Competencies | Relevant Courses |
|---|---|---|---|
| Reading/print awareness (K and Grade 1) | Standard III. Alphabetic Principle; Standard IV. Literacy Development and Practice | Competency 003 (Alphabetic Principle); Competency 004 (Literacy Development) | Emergent literacy |
| Reading/phonological awareness (K and Grade 1) | Standard II. Phonological and Phonemic Awareness | Competency 002 (Phonological and Phonemic Awareness) | Emergent literacy |
| Reading/letter-sound relationships (K and Grade 1) | Standard III | Competency 003 | Emergent literacy |
| Reading/word identification | Standard V. Word Analysis and Decoding | Competency 005 (Word Analysis and Decoding) | Emergent literacy |
| Reading/fluency | Standard VI. Reading Fluency | Competency 006 (Reading Fluency) | Reading courses |
| Reading/variety of texts | Standard VII. Reading Comprehension; Standard X. Assessment and Instruction of Developing Literacy | Competency 007 (Reading Comprehension) | Children's literature; Content area reading; Reading comprehension |
| Reading/vocabulary development | Standard VII | Competency 007 | Content area reading; Reading comprehension |
| Reading/comprehension | Standard VII; Standard X | Competency 007 | Content area reading; Reading comprehension |
| Reading/inquiry/research | Standard VII | Competency 008 (Research and Comprehension Skills in the Content Areas) | Content area reading; Reading comprehension |
| Reading/culture | Standard VII | Competency 007 | Language and culture; Sociology; Reading comprehension |

## 4-8

| TEKS Grades 4 & 5 / TEKS Middle School | Educator Standards | Test Competencies | Relevant Courses |
|---|---|---|---|
| Reading/word identification | Standard II. Foundations of Reading; Standard III. Word Analysis Skills and Reading Fluency; Standard VIII. Assessment of Developing Literacy | Competency 003; Competency 004 | Emergent literacy; Reading comprehension |
| Reading/fluency | Standard III; Standard VIII | Competency 003; Competency 004 | Reading comprehension |

| | | | |
|---|---|---|---|
| Reading/variety of texts | Standard II<br>Standard VIII | Competency 005 | Children's literature<br>Content area reading<br>Reading comprehension |
| Reading/vocabulary development | Standard II<br>Standard III<br>Standard VIII | Competency 002<br>Competency 003<br>Competency 004 | Content area reading<br>Reading comprehension |
| Reading/comprehension | Standard IV. Reading Comprehension | Competency 004<br>Competency 005 | Content area reading<br>Reading comprehension |
| Reading/inquiry/research | Standard IV<br>Standard VIII | Competency 005 | Content area reading<br>Reading comprehension |
| Reading/culture | Standard IV | Competency 004<br>Competency 002 | Language and culture<br>Sociology course<br>Reading comprehension |

## 8-12

| TEKS Grade 8 / TEKS High School | Educator Standards | Test Competencies | Courses |
|---|---|---|---|
| Reading/word identification (Grade 8)<br>Reading/vocabulary development (Grade 8)<br>Reading/word recognition/vocabulary development (High school) | Standard II | Competency 004 | Emergent literacy<br>Reading comprehension |
| Reading/fluency (Grade 8) | Standard II | Competency 004 | Reading comprehension |
| Reading/variety of texts | Standard II<br>Standard III | Competency 004<br>Competency 005 | Computer literacy<br>Content area reading<br>Reading comprehension |
| Reading/comprehension | Standard II<br>Standard III | Competency 004<br>Competency 005 | Content area reading<br>Reading comprehension |
| Reading/inquiry/research | Standard II<br>Standard III | Competency 004<br>Competency 005 | Computer literacy<br>Content area reading<br>Reading comprehension |
| Reading/culture | Standard II | Competency 004 | Language and culture<br>Sociology course<br>Reading comprehension |
| Reading/analysis/evaluation | Standard II<br>Standard III | Competency 004<br>Competency 005 | Reaching comprehension<br>Content area reading |

**comprehension:**   The reader's construction of meaning of a text. Comprehension integrates numerous skills, including but not limited to phonemic awareness, vocabulary knowledge, syntactic knowledge, problem solving, prior knowledge, schema construction, and holistic understanding of the meaning of the text. Comprehension occurs on several levels: *literal, inferential,* and *evaluative.*

**concepts about print:**   An emergent reader's awareness of basic aspects of printed language, such as that English is read from left to right; that some letters are capitals and others lower case; that print includes non-letter symbols, such as punctuation marks; that printed language includes spacing between words and other parts of the text; and that typographical devices such as italics and boldfacing are signals to the reader.

**context clues:**   A *word recognition* strategy in which a reader uses information embedded in a text to decode the meaning of an unfamiliar word.

**decoding:**   The reader's ability to identify and understand unfamiliar words by using *word recognition* strategies such as structural analysis, phonemic analysis, context clues, or syntactic clues. Decoding skills improve as the learner moves from emergent through more proficient levels of reading.

**diagnosis:**   The teacher's ability to explain the underlying causes of miscues and other problems in reading and to accurately describe a developing reader's progress in reading.

**directed reading:**   A reading activity in which the teacher intervenes with introduction of unfamiliar vocabulary, questions, and discussion as readers attempt a new or challenging text assigned by the teacher. Directed reading activities are aimed at helping the learner move toward higher levels of comprehension.

**Drop Everything and Read (DEAR):**   A reading activity in which students and teachers devote a specified time each day to self-selected reading. DEAR is a different label for SSR, Sustained Silent Reading. DEAR and SSR are aimed at developing a lifelong love of reading in students. The underlying assumption is that if students select the texts they want to read, they will enjoy reading and will read on their own. DEAR time is usually very short (15 to 30 minutes) and no follow-up activities are used. In other words, students are not asked to respond orally or in writing to what they have read.

**emergent reader:**   A learner who is in a very early stage of literacy development. An emergent reader knows that the symbols on a page contain meaning but has not yet developed complete *graphophonemic* understanding, has not fully mastered the *alphabetic principle,* has not yet developed *fluency,* and has limited *comprehension* skills. Texts attempted by an emergent reader must be simple in syntax and vocabulary.

**evaluative comprehension:**   One of the three basic levels of comprehension. At this level of comprehension, the reader moves beyond the *literal* and *inferential* levels to connect the information in the passage to his or her own experiences, to find similarities and differences between the text and other texts, and to make judgments about the information and the individuals or characters presented in the passage.

**experiential background:**   Aspects of a reader's life and experiences (personal, academic, or social) that contribute to his or her ability to understand a text. When a teacher helps a learner see connections between his or her life experience and the text being read, the child's comprehension is enhanced.

**fact and opinion:**   An important aspect of *inferential* comprehension. A fact is not subject to argument: A fact provides objective, incontrovertible, sometimes measurable information. Opinion, on the other hand, is a subjective view of a topic, circumstance, or individual. "It's cold in this room" is an *opinion;* "the temperature in this room is 70 degrees" is a *fact.*

**fiction:**   Imaginative literature in which plots, circumstances, and characters convey a theme or central idea. TEKS and educator standards distinguish between fiction and *nonfiction* texts, suggesting that different sets of reading strategies should be applied to the two types of texts.

**figurative language:**   Language in which the meaning is conveyed through indirect rather than literal uses of words and ideas. The ability to recognize and understand figurative language (e.g., simile, metaphor, hyperbole) is a sign of developing literacy. Recognizing how figurative language works in a text is a feature of *inferential* comprehension since it involves understanding based on what is suggested by the language presented in the text. Teachers must remember that sometimes a child's cultural or experiential background may inhibit his or her ability to recognize figurative language.

**fluency:**   The ability to read with ease and understanding at a grade-appropriate rate with a minimal number of miscues. Factors that contribute to fluency include experiential knowledge, reading rate, appropriate intonation, accuracy, effective prediction, confidence, and engagement with the text demonstrated by the reader. When a student reads fluently, the teacher can tell that the child understands what he or she is reading and is not merely reading words on a page.

**generalizing/drawing conclusions:**   A feature of *inferential* comprehension. The reader uses the information in the text to speculate on possible circumstances or outcomes suggested by the situations presented in the text.

**graphic organizer:**   A diagram or visual "scaffolding" intended to help students see connections among concepts in a text. Examples: semantic maps, clustering, webbing, mapping, character webs, T-charts. A graphic organizer may be provided by the teacher or developed by the student, depending on the reader's level of comprehension and specific learning needs. Graphic organizers are highly productive strategies for enhancing comprehension.

**graphophonemic system:**   The correspondence between visual symbols (letters and words) and the sounds they represent.

**high frequency words:**   Words (such as *the, is, of, are, were, in, it, has*) that occur frequently in texts of all kinds. According to reading experts, high frequency words make up half of all the words found in most English texts. For emergent readers, learning to recognize these words significantly aids comprehension skills.

**guided reading:**   Questions and discussion led by the teacher and designed to help students read a new, unfamiliar, or challenging text.

**independent reader:**   A reader who can self-select materials at his or her own reading level and can read with minimal intervention from the teacher.

**independent reading:**   A contrast to directed reading where significant teacher intervention occurs. In independent reading, students manage the reading process on their own. Familiarity with a text, self-selection of the text, and repeated reading of the text are some of the factors that support independent reading. Successful independent reading entails knowing how to apply *metacognitive* skills to manage a challenging text.

**inferential comprehension:**   Usually explained as "reading between the lines." At this level of comprehension, the reader constructs meaning by detecting information suggested rather than literally expressed by the language of the text.

**levels of comprehension:**   Literal, inferential, and evaluative levels of reading. The three levels of comprehension can be used to determine the extent to which a reader is able to understand and respond to a text. A proficient reader relies on all three levels in order to comprehend a text fully and critically; however, young readers need instruction and guidance in learning how to construct meaning at the inferential and evaluative levels.

**literal comprehension:**   A basic level of comprehension in which the reader understands what is *literally* on the page, such as explicitly stated information, words, syntactic structures, main ideas. The reader can restate and paraphrase information but may be unable to demonstrate skills at the higher *inferential* and *evaluative* comprehension levels. Literal comprehension can be traced to actual statements and information in the text while inferential and evaluative information must be deduced by interpreting what the author writes and by relying on information external to the text.

**literature-based instruction:**   Generally refers to teaching approaches other than the *basal reader* approach. Literature-based instruction responds to specific learner readiness and learner needs and thus requires much more active participation by the teacher in the learner's growing reading proficiency.

**literature circles:**   A reading activity in which students are divided into groups (circles) to discuss books they are reading. There are many justifications for setting up literature circles: Students learn how to talk about books they are reading, listen to each other's responses to these books, learn to ask questions about classmates' responses to a text, develop independent reading and response skills. The activity permits a great deal of versatility. Teachers can let reading circles select the books they want to read and discuss, or the discussion can focus on a book the whole class is reading. Literature circles can be used for discussions of fiction as well as nonfiction texts, and they are a productive reading strategy from elementary through high school classrooms. Also known as *reading circles*.

**metacognition:**   The reader's awareness of the thinking skills that he or she is applying during the process of reading. This includes the ability to understand what he or she must do in order to comprehend a text. For example, a sixth grader who recognizes that she is having trouble remembering the information presented in her history book may decide to annotate the text, to take notes, to write chapter summaries, or to read the text when she is not distracted to enhance her comprehension. Metacognitive awareness may tell the reader that something is amiss in his or her reading process. However, metacognitive awareness also enhances the learner's reading pleasure as he or she recognizes how the author's word choice, organization, figurative language, rhetorical choices, and other text components influence the experience of reading.

**miscue:**   A misreading of a text in which the teacher detects a mismatch between the text as it appears and the oral reading the child provides. A miscue should not be considered an error or mistake, but an unexpected or unconventional way of reading the text. The child's oral reading performance indicates that he or she is reading something other than what is actually written in the text. Miscues indicate much about the child's use of phonemic, syntactic, and semantic clues during reading; thus, miscues are good indicators of the child's growing competence in these areas. In addition, miscues reveal the child's ability to perceive an error and to self-correct when the error interferes with comprehension.

**nonfiction:**   Refers to texts based on quantifiable, observed, or factual situations, such as the content of subject-area texts. Nonfiction texts require a different set of reading strategies from those used in reading fiction.

**onset:**   The initial consonant phoneme or digraph (two-consonant blend) in a syllable or word that can be "rhymed" by changing the initial phoneme(s), such as *bat, cat, mat, fat, brat*. Activities involving onset and rime help emergent readers develop *phonemic awareness*.

**oral reading:**   An aspect of reading instruction in which the learner reads a text orally before a small group, the whole class, or the teacher. To be used effectively in promoting reading proficiency, oral reading must be learner-centered, social, and developmentally appropriate. Thus, a text that is read orally by a learner must not include so many unfamiliar words that the reader is unable to demonstrate fluency. It is also important to foster a comfortable environment during oral reading sessions so that students are not intimidated by the teacher or their classmates.

**patterns of organization:**   Organizational principles such as comparison/contrast, cause/effect, and process, that help readers comprehend a text. Each pattern of organization is associated with words that help the reader recognize the pattern and anticipate the presentation of information. For example, a cause-and-effect pattern will use words and phrases such as *reason, cause, outcome, result, motivation, can be attributed to, is traced to, consequence*. Teaching readers to recognize and utilize patterns of organization is an important comprehension strategy.

**phoneme:**   A minimal unit of sound. This is a sound that we can isolate as speakers of a particular language and to which we can assign a meaning-changing variation. For example, the utterances *pit* and *bit* are identical except for the difference in the production of /p/ and /b/—one is produced by constricting the vocal cords, the other by relaxing the vocal cords. This apparently simple variation completely changes the meaning conveyed by the /p/ and /b/ sounds. Consonant blends (e.g., *br, st, tr*) and diphthongs (the vowel sounds in words like *oil* and *made*) are not phonemes since they are produced by combining two minimal sounds. Finally, there are several consonant combinations in English (such as *sh, ch, th*) that are considered phonemes. If you have had no exposure to phonetics in your teacher prep courses, it would be a good idea to read the chapters that cover phonology and phonetics in a linguistics textbook such as Fromkin, Rodman, and Hyams's *An Introduction to Language* (2003) to at least minimally familiarize yourself with important phonetics concepts and with the phonetic alphabet.

**phonemic awareness:**   The ability of emergent readers to distinguish among individual sounds, for example, understanding that *cat* is made up of three separate, minimal sounds (*phonemes*). Phonemic awareness enables emergent readers to make letter-sound correspondences, attempt spelling, recognize onset rimes, develop print awareness, and compose texts of their own.

**prediction:**   The reader's ability to use syntactic, semantic, and phonemic clues in a text to *predict* the meaning of a text, a skill that is vital to developing fluency. Fluent readers do not read individual words as they decode a text; their eyes take in groups of words as they move through the words in a text. The ability to predict meaning in a text grows as the reader's familiarity with phonetic, syntactic, and semantic systems grows, and, eventually, prediction becomes subconscious. The reader does not *consciously* think, "-t-h-e—article—will be followed by a noun or pronoun or adjective-noun combination." But for fluent reading to occur, such prediction must take place. When a reader encounters a text on an unfamiliar subject, prediction is hampered by the reader's inability to use semantic clues effectively. This is why activities such as *semantic mapping* and *prereading* activities are an important part of reading instruction.

**prereading:**   Any activity aimed at stimulating the reader's interest in and eventual comprehension of a new text. A prereading activity must be related to the content of the text. It should be short but it can be a writing activity, an oral language activity, a media literacy activity, or a kinesthetic activity. The point is to activate the child's prior knowledge to enhance comprehension of the text. As children achieve higher levels of comprehension and attempt more challenging texts, prereading may include activities such as previewing the text to gain preliminary information from headings, subheadings, bold-faced words, or marginal comments.

**prior knowledge:**   What a reader knows about the topic or circumstances presented in a text. Teachers should help readers draw on their prior knowledge in order to enhance comprehension. Prior knowledge may be experiential, academic, or teacher-prompted. Prior knowledge is crucial to comprehension. Even if a reader is highly proficient in word recognition, fluency, reading rate, and other aspects of reading, lack of familiarity with a topic can seriously affect the reader's overall comprehension of a text.

**reading circles:**   See *literature circles.*

**reading conference:**   A time of individualized instruction during which a teacher assesses students' progress in reading. During a reading conference, a teacher uses a variety of instructional strategies, including listening to the student read, talking with the student about a book he or she is currently reading, working on specific skills that the student needs to develop, and/or discussing the student's response to a book or shorter text.

**reading workshop:**   A scheduled time when everyone in the class is reading silently and independently. The teacher may designate books that may be read during the workshop, or students may bring their own books from home. The reading workshop could also be used to provide students class time to read books that the whole class is assigned. The workshop may begin with a minilesson on a particular skill the teacher wants students to focus on; it may also end with students' written or oral responses to their reading. The teacher may conduct individual reading conferences to assess students' comprehension and to offer individualized instruction. In contrast to SSR and DEAR, during which students are also reading silently, reading workshop is structured teaching and learning time.

**response log/journal:**   A type of response to assigned or independent reading. Teachers can use response logs to monitor students' comprehension and/or to encourage students to find personal connections with the texts they are reading. The format of response logs varies, but a common approach is to have students write down a short passage (a sentence or two) from the assigned text and then respond to it with a personal or reflective comment. Response logs and journals can be used to prepare students for whole-class or small-group class discussions; they can also be used as an alternative to traditional assessment methods (tests and quizzes).

**rime:**   The phoneme combinations that follow an onset. In the words *rake, cake, make, lake, -ake* is the rime. Activities involving onset and rime help emergent readers develop *phonemic awareness*.

**schema:**   The intellectual "scaffolding" that a reader can use to acquire new knowledge presented in a text. Schema theory is based on the idea that new knowledge must be linked to prior knowledge for learning to occur. As readers grow more proficient, they are able to draw on the appropriate schema to comprehend new texts, but in early stages of reading, the teacher must help the child recognize the schema appropriate to the text. Even proficient adult readers rely on schemas when they encounter texts that contain new information.

**semantic cues:**   The information provided by the meaning of a text that helps readers decode specific elements of the text correctly. For example, in the sentence, "Yesterday, Sammy read the first chapter of *Harry Potter and the Sorcerer's Stone*," *yesterday* provides an important *semantic cue* to the reader: while r-e-a-d may be pronounced "rēd," *yesterday* gives the reader an important clue to the appropriate, context-specific, past-tense pronunciation, "rĕd."

**semantic map:**   A *graphic organizer* aimed at helping readers enhance understanding of a text by linking a new term to words and ideas related to that term. Most of the time a semantic map is constructed by placing the key word in a circle on the page, placing related ideas and words in circles around the main word, and drawing lines connecting the surrounding circles to the central circle. A semantic map may be used as prereading strategy to help the reader anticipate ideas and terms likely to be encountered in the text. In general, a semantic map promotes reading comprehension. *Word cluster* is another term used to describe this strategy.

**sight words:**   Frequently occurring, usually irregularly spelled or irregularly pronounced words that cannot be decoded using *structural* or *phonemic* analysis (such as *the, was, are, of*.) Sight words—whether irregular or regular in spelling—do not need to be decoded because the reader learns to recognize them "on sight." Sight words are a crucial part of early literacy instruction; recognizing sight words significantly contributes to the emergent reader's fluency.

**SQ3R:**   Survey-question-read-recite-respond. A traditional reading strategy aimed at having students apply prereading (survey, question) strategies and literal comprehension strategies (read, recite, review) to enhance their understanding of a text. This is a good strategy for students to use when they will be held responsible for remembering the information in a text (such as in preparing for a test).

**structural analysis:**   A word identification strategy in which developing readers are able to use knowledge of roots and affixes to decode unfamiliar words.

**Sustained Silent Reading (SSR):**   A short period each day (about 15 to 30 minutes), or possibly longer periods at less frequent intervals, when everyone in the class, including the teacher, reads self-selected materials. Different from *reading workshop* during which directed teaching and assessment activities occur. See *Drop Everything and Read (DEAR)*.

**syntactic cues:**   The information provided by sentence structure, inflections, and redundancy that helps young readers decode texts—for example, the knowledge that an article precedes a noun, an *-ed* ending is a verb marker, *-es* is a plural marker, English syntax follows a subject-verb-complement order.

**word cluster:**   Another label for *semantic map*. A word cluster is created by putting a key term in a circle and extending lines from the key term to terms and concepts related to it. Word clusters promote comprehension by familiarizing readers with terms and ideas that are related to a key term in a text.

# Classroom Practices: Reading

Practices that promote productive interactions between learners and teachers are sometimes referred to as good teaching practices. An important part of reading instruction is the teacher's attitude about reading and about teaching reading. Productive teaching practices usually focus on the learner. The following list provides a partial catalog of reading classroom practices based on the language of TEKS, educator standards, and test competencies.

- The reading teacher is aware of individual learners' needs and adjusts instruction and strategies to meet those needs.
- The reading teacher implements authentic assessment practices, integrating instruction with assessment routinely and regularly.
- The reading teacher helps students recognize the importance of literacy for living a full, productive, enjoyable life.
- The reading teacher helps students see that reading is an enjoyable activity that can enrich their lives.
- The reading teacher incorporates technology into the classroom in ways that enhance presentation of reading content and improve students' ability to learn.
- The reading teacher shows students how competence in reading can enhance their performance in all academic areas.
- The reading teacher integrates other language arts into reading instruction.
- The reading teacher varies instructional strategies and practices to maintain learners' interest.
- The reading teacher regularly talks about books that he or she is reading to demonstrate that reading is an important part of life outside the classroom.

Understanding these pedagogical practices could help you recognize the right responses to some objective items that cover reading competencies.

---

REFLECTION FOR YOUR TExES JOURNAL:   In what ways did your teachers implement the practices listed here? What specific literacy learning activities do you remember from your early education?

---

# Familiarity with Grade-Appropriate Reading Materials

Your reading content TExES preparation should include familiarizing yourself with reading materials appropriate to the teaching level for which you are preparing. Your reading and literacy development courses probably included exposure to such texts. However, if you have had no hands-on experience with such texts, you should take some time to familiarize yourself with samples of fiction and nonfiction texts that children at your testing level are likely to encounter in their classrooms. The actual test items might include excerpts from books at the reading level of children you will be teaching. You do not want to spend valuable test-taking time familiarizing yourself with the style and general approach used in grade-level materials, so, as part of your test preparation, learn what your students will be reading.

---

**TEST PREP TIP 8: KNOW THE TEXTS YOUR STUDENTS WILL READ**    As a TExES study strategy, learn what types of texts, both fiction and nonfiction, students at your certification level will be reading.

---

Here are some possibilities for locating and familiarizing yourself with texts that are relevant to your teaching level:

- Visit your Regional Education Service Center. The staff will be very happy to show you copies of the books adopted for content areas (such as social studies, science, or math).
- Your institution may have a library or professional development center for teacher preparation. You will find samples of the books that are used in local public schools.
- If you are an EC-4 certification candidate, you should familiarize yourself with Caldecott and Newbery medal books. Many major bookstores have designated sections for these books. If you read some of these books as a child, don't rely on your memory of the books. You should examine at least a few of them from the perspective of a literacy teacher. You will also find that familiarity with Caldecott and Newbery books will be a major advantage in responding to *literature* test items (this component of the test will be covered in Chapter 4).
- Read some of the articles included in the Selected Resources section of this chapter. Articles that appear in professional reading and ELA journals offer a different type of test preparation from what you learn in textbooks. Your reading course textbooks explain the theory behind good classroom practices. Articles, however, take that theory and show you how it can be applied in real classroom situations. In many cases, the activities described in articles will be similar to the scenarios that will form the basis of the test items on your actual TExES exam.

# Test Item Exercises

Let's examine practice items from the three test levels to see how knowledge of reading terms and reading pedagogical practices can be used to identify the correct response. The items we will analyze are similar in format to the test items you will face on the actual test. Before you look through the practice items, you should review the response strategies presented in Test Prep Tip 6 in Chapter 1.

## EC-4 Exercise

(1) A first grade teacher has noticed that most of her students read haltingly and seem unengaged in the basal reader texts when she listens to them read orally in their reading groups. (2) Which of the following activities would best improve the children's performance during oral reading sessions?

A. Before each oral reading period, students must write a summary of the passage they will read in their reading circles during oral reading time.
B. The teacher takes her students to the school library and tells them to check out a beginning reader's book that they have never read before to read during oral reading time.
C. The teacher designates one day a week as "reader's choice day," when students can read from their favorite books during oral reading time.
D. The teacher distributes a Reading Mistakes Form on which students are to make notes about all the mistakes they hear their classmates make as they read orally.

*Analysis.*   The stem does not specifically mention fluency, but when students read haltingly and with disinterest, they are not reading fluently. The activity the teacher implements must be focused on improving the students' fluency so that the oral reading performances will demonstrate the smooth, confident reading that is characteristic of fluent readers.

- Response A: Writing a summary might seem to be a logical choice since the summary would cause students to become more familiar with the text, and, consequently, the halting reading might be reduced. However, writing a summary is a *writing* rather than oral reading activity. This response should be eliminated because it calls for a language arts activity that does not match the oral reading focus of the stem.
- Response B: Having students read an unfamiliar text during oral reading time is not likely to promote fluency. In fact, such an activity is likely to exacerbate the readers' faltering, disinterested reading. Oral reading is an anxiety-inducing activity for some children, and having to read from an unfamiliar text would probably raise anxiety levels and interfere with reading performance among children who are already having trouble with the basal readers.
- Response C: Reading from a favorite book would be a good choice for an activity designed to enhance fluency. Children are likely to have read the

favorite book over and over and would thus be familiar with the vocabulary as well with the story.

- Response D: While students are supposed to develop techniques for self-evaluation, a Reading Mistakes Form focuses the listeners' attention on error rather than on content. Furthermore, this response focuses on *listening* rather than *performance* and thus moves away from the teaching and learning goal (oral reading improvement) stipulated by the stem.

Response C best matches the specifications established by the item stem.

## 4-8 Exercise

(1) Ms. Vidal, a teacher of grade 5 language arts, has a conversation with Mr. Gonzalez, her students' social studies teacher. (2) He tells her that he is positive the students are not understanding their assigned chapter readings because the class average on the daily homework quizzes is below 50 on a 100-point scale. (3) Which of the following suggestions might Ms. Vidal make to help Mr. Gonzalez assess his students' comprehension of assigned chapters?

A. "You should give your students a set of study questions that they need to answer and be ready to submit to you at the beginning of each class period."
B. "Instead of giving them daily quizzes, you should give them a weekly test every Friday."
C. "You should send a note home to their parents that the parents sign to indicate the child has read the assigned reading."
D. "Instead of a daily quiz, you should have students submit three questions about the chapter content that occur to them as they read the assigned chapter."

*Analysis.* Sentence 1 of the item stem sets up a scenario in which the language arts teacher is conferring with a teacher from another discipline. Sentence 2 identifies a problem in the social studies students' performance on quizzes; you should note that the quizzes are intended to assess the students' comprehension of assigned chapters. Sentence 3 directs the test taker to identify the assessment strategy that will enable Mr. Gonzalez to assess his students' comprehension.

- Response A: Assigning study questions is a traditional, teacher-centered activity. If Mr. Gonzalez is interested in assessing his students' comprehension, this activity is not likely to meet that goal because students typically approach study questions by skimming through the text to find the answers.
- Response B: A weekly test might be a feasible alternative to daily quizzes. Students would have more time to reflect on the information, to reread chapters, and to absorb information covered in class discussions. On the other hand, we could argue that if students are not performing well on daily quizzes, it is not likely that their performance will improve by moving to a full-scale test. Furthermore, in the context of good teaching practices, traditional testing and quizzing is not considered a student-centered activity.

- Response C: This strategy assumes that the parent's signature points to parental involvement in the students' studying, but this strategy, in actuality, does nothing to promote comprehension.
- Response D: Devising questions about the assigned reading is a variation of the reader response journal. The questions will provide a good indication of what students comprehend about the assigned chapter and what they misunderstand. In addition to being student-centered, this activity would provide a basis for in class discussion which would engage students and teacher in authentic discussion of the material in the assigned chapters.

Response D is the best solution to the problem set up in the item stem.

## 8-12 Exercise

(1) Mr. Ling has planned a unit for his ninth-grade English class that will focus on the language of print advertisements. (2) He distributes the following advertising copy from an ad for a gasoline additive:

---

Your high performance sports car was built to be a winner.

Built to lead the pack.

Built to leave the others in the dust.

Don't slow it down with impurities and sludge.

Put Winner's Circle in your gas tank and unleash the beast in your engine.

---

(3) He has students work in groups to analyze the language of the ad. (4) This activity might best help Mr. Ling meet which of the following vocabulary development objectives?

A. To understand how advertisements use sentence fragments to enhance the reader's response to the text
B. To determine the meaning of new words by using context clues
C. To examine how connotations can help a reader construct meaning
D. To explore the fallacies that occur in the language of advertising.

*Analysis.*    Sentences 1 and 2 narrow the activity to the text of a print advertisement, suggesting the focus will be on language rather than on other elements that influence our response to ads (such as graphics, color, font size, and layout, which would make the activity a media literacy activity). Sentences 3 and 4 further focus the activity to a vocabulary development activity; thus, the response must be clearly connected to enhancing students' knowledge of and/or about words.

- Response A: Examining the syntactic deviations that occur in advertisements would probably be a part of a unit on print advertisement, but this response does not meet the vocabulary development focus of the item stem.

- Response B: The copy provided is too concise and too limited to adequately provide context clues, so this would not be a good activity for developing this vocabulary skill.
- Response C: The ad copy is dominated by language that creates images of winning, winners, racing, competition, and animals. Although concise, the text could be used to introduce students to the way connotations shape meaning.
- Response D: Exploring the false claims made in advertisements should be a part of any unit on print advertisements. However, that falls in the category of fallacies and logic rather than vocabulary, and thus does not meet the specifications of the item stem.

Response C best meets the specifications of the item stem.

## Analyzing Reading Items on the Sample Test

Having practiced strategies for using the stem item scenarios to identify the correct response in test item situations, you should look at the sample test items in your TExES Preparation Manual now. Remember that you can identify the reading items by checking the test competencies printed at the bottom of each sample test item. Even if you have attempted these items before reading this chapter, you should look at the items again. If you have studied TEKS, educator standards, and the terms defined in the Glossary of Reading Terms and Concepts, the sample items should be easy to figure out. The process we used in identifying the correct response to the exercises above should be applied in working through sample test items.

---

REFLECTION FOR YOUR TEXES JOURNAL:   Write about your sense of preparedness for the reading portion of the TExES exam you will be taking. Having worked through this chapter, how ready, how confident do you feel about your grasp of the terms and concepts related to reading theory and pedagogy? What areas of reading do you feel least prepared for? How will you continue to prepare for the reading portion of the test?

---

## Chapter Summary

- Study TEKS, educator standards, and test competencies in reading to identify key terms and concepts likely to appear in TExES test items.
- To reinforce your understanding of reading terms, concepts, and teaching practices, correlate TEKS, educator standards, test competencies, and courses relevant to reading using the chart in Figure 2.1.

- Use the glossary to review basic reading terms and concepts, but rely on your textbooks and class notes from reading classes for in-depth explanations of these terms. If you no longer have copies of your reading course textbooks, consult some of the Selected Resources annotated in this chapter.
- Read some fiction and nonfiction texts appropriate to the teaching level for which you are preparing.
- Use your TExES Journal reflections to direct further preparation for your exam.

## Selected Resources: Reading Practice and Pedagogy

Allen, J. (2003). But they still can't (or won't) read! Helping children overcome roadblocks to reading. *Language Arts, 80*(4), 268-274.

> Allen asked her seventh-grade students what they wanted done in the classroom to improve their reading. The consensus was selecting texts that are interesting to students. For the TExES candidate, this article is valuable because of the author's integration of terms and concepts that occur in or are suggested by TEKS and educator standards related to reading (*diverse texts, read alouds, interactive reading, choral reading, fluent reading, independent reading, vocabulary learning, experiential background, high frequency words, text structures*). Allen includes several graphic organizers that can be used to help students develop comprehension of content area textbooks and to increase vocabulary.

Atwell, N. (1998). Learning how to teach reading. Chapter 2 in *In the middle: New understandings about writing, reading, and learning* (2nd ed.). Portsmouth, NH: Heinemann, 27-50.

> Given that Atwell is almost universally cited in discussions of reading workshop applications in ELA classrooms, TExES candidates should find this chapter illuminating. TExES candidates should examine and think about Atwell's "Twenty-one lessons teachers demonstrate about reading" in the context of TEKS and educator standards. In this chapter, Atwell adeptly integrates terminology associated with teaching reading with her own metaphors about teaching reading and with stories about real students in real reading classroom scenarios.

Bell, S. (2004). Transforming seniors who don't read into graduates who do. *English Journal 93*(5), 36-41.

> Although Bell's focus is to show how twelfth-grade teachers can prepare their students for college-level reading tasks, this article has relevance for TExES candidates in its application of reading concepts and activities at the upper high school level. Key terms such as *SSR, paraphrasing, main ideas, comprehension, tone, inference, fluency, scaffolding, reluctant readers,* and *critical reading skills* are used throughout the article. Bell's experience as a Texas educator makes her classroom practices particularly applicable to TExES exam preparation.

Fromkin, V., Rodman, R., & Hyams, N. (2003). *An introduction to language* (7th ed.). Boston: Wadsworth.

> Several chapters in this widely adopted book offer valuable information on technical aspects of reading: Chapter 3, Morphology: The Words of Language; Chapter 6, Phonetics: The Sounds of Language; Ch. 7, Phonology: The Sound Patterns of Language. Knowing how to analyze words morphologically and phonetically is a crucial skill in teaching reading.

Lause, J. (2004). Using reading workshop to inspire lifelong readers. *English Journal 93*(5), 24-30.

> Describes an adaptation of Nancie Atwell's reading workshop in ninth- and tenth-grade classes. [Atwell's workshop, detailed in *In the middle: New understandings about writing,*

*reading, and learning* (1998) was originally set in middle school.] Lause targets students who see reading merely as an academic exercise and have no independent love of reading. Her workshop adaptation combines required reading of seven literary classics with self-selected daily reading. TExES candidates should find this article valuable for its use of reading terms and concepts in real-world teaching situations. In addition, the article shows how reading instruction is implemented at the high school level.

Leu, D. J., Jr., & Kinzer, C. K. (2003). *Effective literacy instruction K-8: Implementing best practice* (5th ed.). Upper Saddle River, NJ: Merrill Prentice-Hall.

This is an excellent resource for the ELA/Reading TExES candidate. The book includes definitions (key terms are highlighted throughout the book), sample student work, model lessons, practical teaching strategies, and clear explanations of all aspects of literacy instruction. A particularly valuable feature of the book is the authors' integration of technological resources into literacy instruction—they provide examples and explanations of numerous technology applications including teacher-prepared Web pages, email applications, and Internet applications.

McGee, L. M., & Richgels, D. J. (2004). *Literacy's beginnings: Supporting young readers and writers* (4th ed.). Boston: Pearson Education.

The EC-4 TExES candidate will find this book a "must have" resource. The authors cover all aspects of literacy from preliteracy stages through early elementary grades. The combination of explanations firmly grounded in theory and sound practice, actual examples of children's literacy products, and classroom scenarios will contribute significantly to the TExES candidates' understanding of terminology in TEKS and educator standards. Key terms appear in bold face throughout the book, an important feature for TExES candidates who might be searching for specific definitions and/or explanations of particular terms. The authors devote considerable attention to the role of the child's family in the development of literacy; the TExES candidate should note that this is a recurrent concept in educator standards.

Rasinski, T. V., & others. (Eds.). (2000). *Developing reading-writing connections: Strategies from* The Reading Teacher. Newark, DE: International Reading Association.

This is a collection of 42 articles on reading and writing teaching activities from *The Reading Teacher,* a publication of the International Reading Association. The articles are highly instructive for EC-4 TExES candidates because the authors consistently use terms relevant to TEKS and educator standards in the context of describing creative, student-centered classroom activities.

Richards, M. (2000). Be a good detective: Solve the case of oral reading fluency. *The Reading Teacher* 53(7), 534-539.

Richards makes a strong case for making oral reading fluency a stronger component of reading instruction rather than a by-product of reading instruction. Important TExES-relevant terms explained and illustrated in this article include *oral reading fluency, reading rate, prosody, comprehension, direct instruction, modeling, repeated reading, paired oral reading, choral reading,* and numerous other terms.

Thomas, C. (2000). From engagement to celebration: A framework for passionate reading. *Voices from the Middle 8*(2), 16-25.

Thomas begins by vividly describing her passion for reading and for books, an attitude that is essential for helping our students become lifelong readers. She describes class activities for fostering in students an appreciation for nonfiction texts, which, according to Thomas, students usually equate with dry academic texts. Thomas' extended explanations of how she incorporates specific nonfiction texts into her sixth-grade curriculum should be helpful to the TExES candidate in understanding the difference between fiction and nonfiction texts. TExES-relevant terms that appear in this article include *literature circles, story map, storyboard, reader response, oral reading of poetry, collaboration.*

# CHAPTER

# 3

# Writing

## Process, Practice, and Pedagogy

The writing component of all ELA TExES levels ranks second in terms of coverage and emphasis after the reading component. Whether you are testing at the EC-4, 4-8, or 8-12 level, you will need to demonstrate considerable familiarity with aspects of writing, including current writing theory and pedagogy, best practices for implementing writing instruction, grammar and language use, and technology applications in the teaching of writing. As you review the terms and concepts related to writing, you might want to think about your own writing process so that you can put the theory and pedagogy we will discuss in this chapter into a tangible context. If you have had a writing methods course, chances are good that you have spent some class time talking about your own writing process. So, at this point, stop and ask yourself the following questions:

- What do I do when I face a writing task?
- Can I identify repeatable steps I take when I have a writing task to complete?
- What makes me feel like writing?
- What situations interfere with my writing process?
- What do I like best about writing?
- What do I like least about writing?
- What classroom activities and teacher attitudes have been conducive to my progress in writing?

REFLECTION FOR YOUR TExES JOURNAL: Respond to some or all of the questions listed above. If you have done similar exercises in your advanced composition or writing methods courses, try to find essays or other class materials in which you recorded your responses to these questions.

# An Overview of Writing Theory and Pedagogy

We'll start our writing review by establishing basic understandings about what happens when we teach writing and about what we mean when we talk about writing in the ELA classroom. So, let's look at a working definition of writing in the context of teaching language arts.

---

**WRITING: A WORKING DEFINITION**  Writing is the component of language arts that focuses on helping students construct messages to be read or heard by an audience. Effective writing encompasses a vast variety of elements (e.g., focus, unity, coherence, language use, rhetoric, style) that enable the writer to achieve his or her purposes while focusing on the audience's response to the message.

---

At the core of contemporary approaches to teaching writing is the understanding that writing is a *process* and it is best taught as such. This means that the practices we implement in helping students progress through the process of writing are as important as the eventual product of writing. Because of the prevailing theoretical and pedagogical emphasis on writing as a process, we also need to recognize that writing is considered a multistage process, with basic stages that include (1) preparation (or prewriting or discovery), (2) drafting, (3) revision, (4) editing, and (5) publication. While these are the terms typically associated with the stages of the writing process, the specific textbooks you end up using when you teach may use different and/or additional terms. For the purposes of TExES preparation, we will use the five terms we just mentioned because these are reflected in TEKS, educator standards, and test competencies.

Effective implementation of writing theory and pedagogy in the ELA classroom is based on several fundamental attitudes toward writing such as those listed below. Many of the terms included in the list will be defined, explained, or illustrated in the glossary later in this chapter.

- A *writing workshop* environment seems to be the best approach for developing confident, competent writers.
- Effective writing takes time, so significant, frequent segments of class time should be allotted for writing activities. In practical terms, this means you should allot 30 minutes or more several times a week to writing if you want to see progress in your students' writing competence. Occasionally, a series of consecutive class periods devoted to writing might be useful for helping students move through the writing process completely during a particular writing task.
- The teacher should function as a *coach* who recognizes effective behaviors and competencies and helps student writers work at overcoming problems in writing.

- Grammar instruction should occur in the context of the students' own writing.
- Grammar instruction should be focused on helping students develop competence and confidence in formulating their responses to specific writing tasks.
- The teacher should demonstrate that he or she is a writer and enjoys writing. This attitude goes a long way toward developing in students an appreciation of writing.

REFLECTION FOR YOUR TExES JOURNAL: Think about your best experiences in writing classes or in classes in which writing has been a significant component. To what extent did your instructors implement the practices listed above? How did those practices contribute to your learning experience in those classes?

## Coordinating TEKS, Educator Standards, and Test Competencies in Writing

Figure 3.1 correlates the various components of TEKS, educator standards, and test competencies related to writing.

Let's designate blue as the color for highlighting and flagging writing components of your TExES preparation. So, before you move on, use the chart to identify and mark in blue TEKS headings, educator standards, and test competencies related to writing—and take time now to look through these components, noting key terms and identifying terms you need to define.

REFLECTION FOR YOUR TExES JOURNAL: Take time to read and study the components of the Writing Study Chart applicable to your certification level. In your TExES journal, jot down key terms and, particularly, terms you don't recognize. Also jot down questions about writing theory and practice that occur to you as you read through writing TEKS, educator standards, and competencies.

## A Glossary of Selected Writing Terms and Concepts

In the writing category, there seems to be greater consistency and repetition of terms and concepts across all grades than in any other language arts TExES. For example, from as early as grade 1, TEKS include student expectations regarding audience awareness, drafting, and writing purposes, as well as others, expectations that are reiterated through all TEKS levels. Try not to dismiss any of the terms and concepts below as irrelevant to your TExES exam because most of the terms in fact are applicable to all three certification levels.

**FIGURE 3.1   Writing Study Chart**

| EC-4 | | | |
| --- | --- | --- | --- |
| **TEKS K-4** | **Educator Standards** | **Test Competencies** | **Relevant Courses** |
| Writing/spelling/penmanship<br>Writing/penmanship/capitalization/<br>　punctuation<br>Writing/composition<br>Writing/inquiry/research<br>Writing/purposes<br>Writing/writing processes<br>Writing/spelling<br>Writing/grammar/usage<br>Writing/evaluation<br>Writing/connections | Standard VIII.<br>Development of Written<br>Communication<br>Standard IX.<br>Writing Conventions | Competency 009 (Writing<br>Conventions)<br>Competency 010<br>(Development of Written<br>Communication) | Emergent literacy<br>Literacy development<br>Writing methods<br>Freshman English |

| 4-8 | | | |
| --- | --- | --- | --- |
| **TEKS Grades 4 and 5**<br>**TEKS Middle School** | **Educator Standards** | **Test Competencies** | **Relevant Courses** |
| Writing/purposes<br>Writing/penmanship/capitalization/<br>　punctuation/spelling<br>Writing/spelling<br>Writing/grammar/usage<br>Writing/writing processes<br>Writing/evaluation<br>Writing/inquiry/research<br>Writing connections | Standard V.<br>Written Language | Competency 006 (Written<br>Language—Writing<br>Conventions)<br>Competency 007 (Written<br>Language—Composition) | Emergent literacy<br>Literacy development<br>Writing methods<br>Freshman English |

| 8-12 | | | |
| --- | --- | --- | --- |
| **TEKS Grade 8**<br>**TEKS High School** | **Educator Standards** | **Test Competencies** | **Courses** |
| Writing/purposes<br>Writing/penmanship/capitalization/<br>　punctuation/spelling<br>Writing/grammar/usage<br>Writing/processes<br>Writing/evaluation<br>Writing/inquiry/research<br>Writing/connections<br>Writing/usage/conventions/spelling<br>Writing/analysis | Standard V<br>Standard VI<br>Standard VII | Competency 003<br>Competency 008<br>Competency 009 | Emergent literacy<br>Literacy development<br>Writing methods<br>Freshman English |

**audience:**   A component of almost any writing task. ELA teachers are frequently criticized for not creating realistic audiences for student writing, so the TEKS requirements related to audience awareness should alert teachers to the problem of specifying an audience. Audience awareness calls for role-playing on the part of the writer and for creativity on the part of the teacher in devising writing tasks that include a specific, authentic audience.

**author's chair:**   A classroom activity intended to develop students' audience awareness (and perhaps to simultaneously develop oral language skills). There is no fixed method for implementing author's chair activities. Usually, one student sits in the "author's chair" and shares his or her writing with the rest of the class. Feedback, of course, is a vital part, but in author's chair settings, the feedback should be aimed at supporting the author rather than at improving the text.

**brainstorming:**   A common, much used prewriting strategy in which the writer or a writing group lists ideas related to the writing topic. Brainstorming works best if the brainstormers do not censor their ideas and if they stick to words and phrases (as opposed to sentences) in order to make the process happen quickly. It is important not to confuse brainstorming with other prewriting strategies, such as webbing or freewriting. The brainstorming product should look like a list of words and phrases and should be completed quickly. The brainstormed list can be categorized into topics and turned into a rough outline, or it can be used to identify a single, refined subtopic relevant to the writing topic. Brainstorming seems to work best when students work in small groups or whole class contexts because of the very social nature of the activity. However, it can also be used productively by individual writers to generate ideas related to the assigned writing topic.

**coherence:**   The features of a text that contribute to the general "togetherness" of the text. Coherence begins with attention to the unity of the central idea, but coherence can be enhanced by rhetorical choices such as repetition of sentence patterns, maintaining a consistent point of view throughout the text, focusing on the major idea in body paragraphs, and repetition of key terms throughout appropriate segments of the text. While transitional sentences and expressions contribute to coherence, these alone cannot create coherence.

**collaboration in writing:**   Cooperation among one or more students in the process and production of a writing assignment. Collaboration can be formal as when a group is assigned a writing task and all group members contribute equally to the outcome, or it may be less formal, as when students collaborate during peer editing or writing workshop activities. Collaboration is generally recognized as a good teaching strategy since it promotes socialization during the writing process.

**concept of word:**   Applies primarily to emergent readers and writers who must learn that words have boundaries, that letters and syllables are used to compose words, that in writing, words are separated by space, and other similar concepts. Let's say a 4-year-old child draws a picture, writes the letter $L$ at the bottom of the picture, and then "reads" you what she wrote: "Goliath was a giant. David killed Goliath." At this point, the child's writing does not demonstrate concept of word since she is using the letter $L$ to signify several sentences and many words. With older writers, concept of word could be used to explain otherwise inexplicable errors when they attempt to write for the first time a word they have heard and used orally but have never used in writing, for example, writing "day view" instead of "debut." Clearly, there are other problems involved with errors such as these, but the problem could at least be partly explained by the writer's inability to detect the word boundaries and to translate the sounds into the syllables and words that make sense in the context of the idea being discussed.

**conferencing:**   Considered by many writing theorists and practitioners to be the most effective strategy for teaching writing. Conferencing can be one-on-one between student and teacher in a formal setting (as when the teacher schedules conferences with students to go over drafts for specific assignments) or informal and impromptu (as when the teacher works with students as questions arise during writing workshop sessions). Conferences can be long (30 minutes or longer) or very short (30 seconds). Conferencing approaches are varied: The teacher may make pointed suggestions for changes, the teacher may ask students to read a draft aloud and have the student self-correct; the teacher may invite the student to ask questions about the draft, or the teacher may ask questions that lead the student toward discovery of better approaches to the task.

**conventions of written English:** The typographical, formatting, and mechanical "rules" that we have agreed are necessary for the production of readable written texts. Some examples of conventions include indenting paragraphs; centering the title at the top of the page; capitalizing the first word of each sentence; using terminal punctuation; observing margins; boldfacing, italicizing, or underlining for emphasis; and paginating. As readers, we automatically expect that conventions have been observed, so one way of "convincing" students of the importance of using conventions of written English is to point out that they are a vital aspect of *audience awareness*.

**documentation styles:** The set of guidelines established for documentation in widely used style sheets, such as The Modern Language Association (MLA), the Chicago Manual, the American Psychological Association (APA). In TEKS, documentation is incorporated into the writing/research sections.

**drafting:** The stage of the writing process when the writer begins to shape his or her ideas into sentences and paragraphs that are intended to achieve a specific purpose and develop a specific thesis or topic sentence. While some types of prewriting elicit sentences and paragraphs, prewriting differs from drafting in that prewriting for the most part is tentative and unorganized. Drafting, on the other hand, generally begins after the writer has discovered and settled on a focal point. In process writing, students are generally encouraged to produce multiple drafts as they work toward completion of the writing task. When students use word processors to produce drafts, teachers should encourage students to save the various drafts as different files in order to prevent premature deletion of sections of the draft that the writer may want to integrate later in the drafting process.

**edited American English:** The form of written English that generally observes accepted rules of usage and conventions of English. Edited American English may be informal (student essays) or highly formal (professional writing). It is important to note that the term is *edited* American English, which strongly implies that the deliberate application of rules of usage requires reflection and time.

**editing:** One of the stages of the writing process. Editing occurs after all major global revision has been completed. Changes that are made at this point should not affect holistic concerns (such as development, focus, organization, tone). For the most part, changes made during the editing stage should be local: That is, they should be sentence level or lower. Typical changes that occur during editing are spelling corrections, insertion of punctuation, word substitutions, and minor sentence structure changes. It is important to recognize that if editing occurs too early in the writing process—for example, during drafting—it can interfere with the writer's flow of ideas. Furthermore, it is pointless to encourage students to make superficial corrections and changes during early drafting because later drafting may prove that the structures to which changes were made are now irrelevant or need substantive holistic change. If writers feel uncomfortable about deferring editing until the very end of the writing process, we can encourage them to embed signals in the text about minor structures they want to change later (for example, they could highlight a word for which they want to check spelling or place an asterisk in the margin of a sentence whose structure or rhythm seems suspect). TEKS treats editing as a stage separate from revision, and that is an important distinction for prospective TExES candidates to make.

**editing and word processing:** A productive means of encouraging students to improve their writing. The most familiar word processing tool is the spell check function, but it is important to teach students how to use this so that they don't automatically assume a word is misspelled when in fact it is only misused or so that they do not hit the "ignore" command when they think they have spelled a word correctly. Other useful word processing tools include the preview function, which can be used to help students check on overly long or inappropriately short paragraphing; the word count, which can help them meet length specifications of a writing assignment; the readability statistics, which can be used to encourage sentence combining and integration of more sophisticated vocabulary; and the cut and paste feature, which can be used to create coherence or improve the logical progression of major ideas.

**evaluating student writing:**    An important tool for improving student writing. Teachers need to be aware of the many aspects of evaluation, including a correlation between the evaluation and the type of assignment; pre-established criteria for evaluation; the impact of error counting; the use of marginal and end comments; the way the writing process is implemented in the classroom; the difference between formative and summative evaluation; and even the use of red ink. Evaluation becomes a means of improving student writing when the teacher helps students see what has been done effectively in a specific writing task and what needs improvement. While most writers appreciate praise from an evaluator, unspecific praise ("Terrific!") is not likely to promote growth in writing competence because the writer does not know what the praise refers to. Teachers should, therefore, be specific about what the writer has done effectively ("Good job of devising a thesis statement that clearly sets up the proposition you will address in your essay"). For the pragmatic purpose of preparing for TExES, we are focusing only on classroom evaluation of student writing, where the teacher determines what evaluation method will be used. TEKS does not address programmatic evaluation where schoolwide, district-level, or state-level evaluation of writing calls for different evaluation approaches.

**features of effective writing:**    The aspects of a written text that are generally recognized by writing teachers and writing professionals as essential to the effectiveness of the text. There are no absolute features of effective writing, but there are some general categories that we can agree are important in most types of writing, such as focus, organization, coherence, development, attention to the writing task, language use, grammar, and mechanics.

**forms or genres of expository writing:**    Terms used to encompass a broad variety of types of writing. There is little consistency in writing theory and practice about these terms, but discussing that inconsistency is beyond the scope of this book. It may help to begin by thinking of what *is not* expository writing: argumentation or persuasion, creative writing, and informative writing. Expository writing very generally may be thought of as writing that makes a point that expresses the writer's personal view on an issue or topic. Thus, much writing we do in our classes is covered by this term. While expository writing may include informative, creative, and persuasive aspects, if those aspects become the distinguishing feature or focal purpose of the writing, then it is not expository.

**freewriting:**    A writing activity intended to help students generate ideas quickly and prolifically. There are many variations of freewriting, but it usually involves a short, timed writing session during which students write on a self-selected or teacher-assigned topic. Freewriting should be written in more or less conventional sentences and paragraphs in contrast to *brainstorming,* which is primarily a listing process. Sometimes freewriting involves just writing about whatever comes to mind. Usually, freewriting is integrated into the writing process as a *prewriting* strategy.

**grammar:**    One of the many components of English language arts. When we talk about grammar, we are actually talking about several different things: our intuitive knowledge of the rules of English (e.g., phonetics, morphology, syntax, and semantics), the various approaches to grammar (traditional, structural, generative-transformational), the rules of usage ("don't end a sentence with a preposition"), and "school" grammar (e.g., parts of speech, sentence types, comma rules). In the TEKS writing categories on grammar and usage, specific grammatical elements are mentioned, such as subject-verb agreement, punctuation, and gerund usage. It would be a good test preparation strategy to look over all writing/grammar/usage TEKS sections in the grade levels applicable to your TExES exam to ensure that you are familiar with the specific grammar terms mentioned in those categories. If you feel insecure about being able to identify specific types of grammar problems (such as comma splices, run-ons, fragments, predication problems, inconsistent point of view), you should look through a good handbook to refresh your knowledge in such areas. *The New Century Handbook* (Hult & Huckin, 2002), included in the Selected Resources in this chapter, is a good choice for reviewing grammar terms and concepts.

**Internet:**   A significant resource in teaching writing or developing writing abilities. Think of the Internet both as a means of helping students meet writing/research TEKS expectations and as a potential venue for nonprint texts (as in production of Web pages).

**invented spelling:**   The attempts by young writers to "translate" into writing the sounds of words. Invented spelling can be phonetic (as when a child spells *turtle* as t-r-l) or transitional, indicating that the child is beginning to apply orthographic rules (as in the spelling of *turtle* as t-e-r-l). We usually think of invented spelling as being a characteristic of young writers whose literacy skills are still developing; however, invented spellings occur in the writing of much older students whenever they attempt to integrate into their writing words that they have heard but possibly have never seen in writing, as when a high school student writes "The whole situation deteriorated into caious" where *chaos* is spelled inventively as c-a-i-o-u-s.

**journals/journal writing:**   A versatile, productive writing activity for all levels of students. There is actually no single way of defining journals, but journal writing can be defined through some general characteristics. (1) Journals are collections of student writing entries that are produced regularly either in class or out of class. (2) Journals should not be graded or evaluated since the point of journaling is to elicit reflective or expressive writing. (3) Journals may be used to stimulate thinking about specific topics that will be integrated into ELA assignments (e.g., essay writing, literature, current events discussion).

**minilesson:**   A short, concentrated teaching presentation on a specific topic. A minilesson is intended to focus students' attention on a very specific element of language arts—for example, the thesis, semicolons, or plural formation when a word ends in y. Minilessons should be only about 15 to 20 minutes long and should include opportunities for students to interact with the teacher during the presentation. The "mini" aspect of the minilesson is important: It is not supposed to be a full-fledged lesson on the topic, nor it is supposed to be the introductory lesson on the topic. It is primarily designed to help students manage a specific language arts topic for which a context has been established in previous lessons.

**models:**   Sample texts used to illustrate specific types of writing, particular rhetorical and/or grammatical structures in writing, modes of development, or other topics. The underlying assumption in the use of models is that students will emulate the models and thereby improve their own writing competence.

**organization:**   The feature of writing that enables a reader to follow the text without confusion. Globally, organization includes a strong thesis or focal point and paragraphs that clearly address the proposition or opinion presented in the thesis. Traditional topic sentences that establish the focus of each paragraph are an important element of organization. Organization can also refer to specific strategies such as definition, comparison/contrast, cause/effect, illustration, or argument.

**orthography:**   The rules and principles associated with spelling. Knowledge of orthographic rules enables young writers to produce texts that are comprehensible to readers other than themselves. Many orthographic rules are learned as the child learns to read and gradually discovers the patterns of English spelling. For example, a young reader will gradually realize that English syllables must include a vowel sound but do not always include consonants. Other rules, such as plural formation rules, require focused attention and guidance from the teacher. The invented spellings a child produces are good indicators of the way the learner is processing orthographic rules.

**parts of speech:** Noun, verb, pronoun, adjective, adverb, conjunction, preposition, interjection. You should be able to identify parts of speech in context in order to help students write effectively. In analyzing student writing, it is sometimes important to trace particular writing problems to misunderstanding of the way parts of speech are used. It is also important to recognize that parts of speech are not absolute, that a particular word can be categorized as several parts of speech depending on how it is used in a sentence. For example, an exaggerated statement such as "The *baby* in the *baby* buggy was *babied* excessively by the *baby's* mother" could be used to demonstrate to students how "baby" functions as several different parts of speech in this sentence.

**peer editing:** A class activity that involves having students respond to each other's drafts during the writing process. Peer editing may be general or highly specific. Students may be asked to respond personally to a classmate's draft, or they may be asked to respond to specific elements of the draft. Some teachers use detailed peer editing worksheets to help students learn to respond to others' writing. Peer editing helps students understand that writing is a social activity.

**phonics and writing:** The connection between the sounds of language and the orthographic representation. For emergent readers and writers, the connection between phonics and writing is important. Students need to be aware that the sounds of words are not always represented by the same letter combinations. For example, young writers need to learn that the *f* sound can be represented in writing by the letters *f, ph,* and *gh.* A teacher can tell much about a students' developing literacy by noting the rationale behind the *invented spellings* that the student produces.

**portfolio evaluation:** An approach to evaluation of writing in which students play a major role in selecting the work to be evaluated. Although portfolio evaluation is manifested in many different permutations, it basically involves having students write a series of assignments throughout a grading period (six weeks, nine weeks, semester). The teacher works with the students through their writing process but delays formal evaluation of the finished products until the end of the grading period. Students produce a portfolio of their work based on the teacher's pre-established requirements for the portfolio. For example, the teacher may require that one personal essay, one thesis-and-support essay, and one on-demand essay be submitted in the portfolio. Portfolio evaluation also usually includes a reflective piece in which students discuss what they learned about writing as they prepared their portfolio. As the term is used in the context of evaluation of writing, a portfolio is not simply a folder in which all the student's work for a particular session has been collected.

**prewriting:** The first stage of the writing process during which students generate ideas or research a topic. Prewriting strategies include discussion, thinking, researching, brainstorming, webbing, freewriting, outlining, and other similar activities designed to help students identify material that might be used in completing the writing task. Teachers must understand that not all prewriting strategies work for all students. For example, some students may find freewriting a very productive prewriting strategy, but other students may find this strategy too unfocused for their thinking processes. In addition, very young writers need other types of prewriting strategies, such as drawing or talking.

**publishing:** The final stage of the writing process. Publication can take many forms: The class may produce a booklet showcasing their responses to a particular writing assignment; students may present their essays orally in an author's chair setting; or the teacher may tack all the essays on the bulletin board for students to read at their leisure.

**purpose:** The rationale that motivates the production of a particular written text. The concept of purpose in writing is presented in a variety of ways in the TEKS context. In general, the writer's purpose influences all aspects of the writing task: tone, diction, rhetorical choices, form, and so on. Recognizing one's purpose also impacts audience awareness and influences the choices writers make in order to reach the audience. Typical purposes include to inform, to persuade, to entertain, or to express.

**quickwrite:**  Informal writing that, as the term suggests, occurs quickly and briefly. Quickwrites have a variety of applications in classrooms at all teaching levels: They can be used to elicit response to a literary or nonfiction text or written commentary on a class activity or class discussion. Response is the focal feature of quickwrites, which means that these are not formally evaluated. Quickwrites suggest spontaneity, brevity, and a high level of writer confidence (because the writer is thinking about the response rather than the form and conventions of the written text).

**recursiveness:**  The feature of the writing process that enables a writer to return to an earlier stage of the process in order to change some aspect of the writing. If we say that the writing process is recursive, we are also saying that it is not strictly linear (where one step is completed absolutely and unchangeably before the writer moves on to the next step). Emphasizing the recursiveness of the writing process should help reduce the anxiety that some student writers feel when they are faced with a writing task.

**research process:**  A specific application of the writing process. Since the writing-related TEKS include a writing/research/inquiry section, it is important to familiarize yourself with the approach to research presented by TEKS. A significant aspect of the TEKS approach to research is that the process begins with setting up research questions to investigate. Research involves critical thinking about a topic as well as strategies for collecting, evaluating, and presenting the results of research. Integrating technology into the research process is an aspect of the TEKS approach to the research process. Such integration ranges from the use of Internet sources to the use of electronic media for presenting the results of research.

**revising:**  One of the stages of the writing process. While revising may occur throughout the composing process, it is important for student writers to recognize that revision is a distinct stage during which global and local changes are made to the document being composed. Revision involves deletion, addition, substitution, repositioning, and sometimes, reversion to an earlier writing stage. At one extreme, during revision, a writer may discover that the focus of the paper is so far removed from the requirements of the writing task that it is necessary to go back to the prewriting stage and "start over." At the other extreme is the situation that exists when a writer consistently and effectively revises as he or she drafts, and the revision stage more or less reaffirms the choices and changes the writer made during the multiple drafting stages. It is important to differentiate between *editing* and *revising*. Editing, as noted in the glossary entry, involves more or less superficial changes.

**self-evaluation of writing:**  An important aspect of helping students become independent, confident writers. Probably the most frequently used strategy for self-evaluation is the revision worksheet or checklist that guides the writer through a series of questions or checkpoints that require critical assessment of the draft. Such worksheets invite the writer to examine everything from the existence of the thesis to the structure of sentences.

**self-initiated/self-motivated writing:**  Writing initiated by the student writer to fulfill goals other than complying with a classroom assignment. This may be a journal that the student is writing on his or her own, poetry, short stories, reflective pieces, and so on. Writing that is assigned, even if it is a journal that will not be formally graded, cannot be considered self-motivated. Self-motivated writing includes submissions to the school literary magazine, service on the school newspaper, letters to the editor, submissions to national student writing journals, such as NCTE's *Teen Ink*.

**sentence patterns/types:**  Simple, compound, complex, compound-complex. To help students improve their writing style and to help students avoid certain types of syntax problems, teachers must know what the basic sentence patterns are. While students do not need to be able to identify the types of sentences they are writing, it is almost imperative that teachers know how to help students produce sentences that enhance their syntactic fluency and that are constructed using appropriately applied sentence-combining strategies.

**spelling:** The category of English language arts that involves application of orthographic rules and knowledge in production of written texts. While spelling is an important area of language arts, we should strive to place it in an appropriate context as we guide our students through language instruction. The easiest but not necessarily the most effective way to teach spelling is to give students word lists on which they are tested periodically. Unfortunately, there is no agreement on the best way to teach spelling, but in the context of TExES preparation accurate spelling is considered an important aspect of effective writing as demonstrated by the inclusion of spelling-related TEKS through grades K-English IV (grade 12). Teachers are better able to help students solve their spelling problems if they are able to identify the problem through error analysis. For example, a student who consistently confuses the "spelling" of *its/it's, their/they're/there,* or *to/two/too* has a different type of problem from the student who writes *use to* instead of *used to* or the student who writes *cloths* instead of *clothes.* So, helping students spell correctly means knowing how to explain spelling conventions to students.

**stages of writing:** Prewriting, drafting, revising, editing, and publishing. Teaching writing as a multistage process means that we must allot substantive portions of class time for writing and that we recognize the need to provide realistic deadlines for completing writing tasks. In a process writing classroom, the teacher functions as a coach, working with students throughout the writing process.

**standard English usage:** Sometimes used as a variation of the term *edited American English;* however, *standard English usage* has as an underlying tenet the understanding that there are numerous varieties of American English but that, for ease of communication, *standards* of usage should be observed. Equally important is the understanding that no one variety of English is superior to others. In areas where many of our students speak a variety of English that is significantly different from standard American English, it is important that we value our students' own language and that we guide them toward using standard English usage in appropriate situations without implying that their own language is deficient or inferior.

**style:** The writer's choices in syntax and diction. As a student of literature, you are able to quantify the stylistic differences between William Faulkner and Ernest Hemingway: Faulkner creates deeply embedded, lengthy sentences while Hemingway is noted for his pithy almost laconic sentences. Style is related to sentence length and sentence structure. Students need to be guided toward making stylistic choices that are appropriate for the intended audience and for the intended presentation. For example, students should be informed that long, involved sentences are not appropriate in oral presentations because listeners are likely to lose track of the point of the sentence. Similarly, the style of sentences that we appreciate in literature are inappropriate for a research paper in a history class because of the different purposes in those writing tasks.

**syntax:** The area of linguistics that deals with sentence structure and the rules for constructing sentences. Knowledge of the way syntactic choices affect writing is vital to a language arts teacher's ability to help students improve their writing. While syntax is fundamentally an aspect of grammar (sentence types), it is also a versatile rhetorical tool for all writers. Syntactic choices contribute to the style, the mood, the tone, the density, the complexity, and the meaning of a text.

**technology and writing:** The integration of computer technology into the teaching and production of writing. If we have our students work regularly in a computer classroom, we are integrating technology into writing through the use of word processing tools, integration of other programs into word processing programs, and the use of Internet resources, for example. Technology should be used not for its own sake but instead for helping students become more proficient writers.

**voice:**  The quality of writing that enables the reader to detect a "personality" behind the words. We can encourage students to develop voice in their writing by creating writing tasks that allow students to become engaged with the task. That engagement causes student writers to feel enthusiastic about the assignment and to make rhetorical and stylistic choices designed to impact a reader. We can help students understand what voice means by examining models and discussing how specific strategies (such as diction choices, rhetorical sentence patterns, humor, and irony) contribute to voice.

**word processing:**  A tool that can be used to help student writers in various ways: to facilitate the production of drafts, to encourage significant revision, to revise and edit using editing tools (such as grammar checks, spell checks, word counts, and readability guides), and to prepare a text for publication.

**writer's block:**  A very real problem for many writers. In general terms, writer's block means the inability to transform the ideas conceived during *prewriting* into organized text during *drafting*. Writer's block manifests itself in many ways. In classroom writing situations, when a student is unable to produce more than one or two sentences in a significant writing period and this behavior persists throughout numerous writing sessions, the teacher could legitimately conclude that this student has writer's block. Professional writers reduce writer's block by getting away from the writing task for a while or by writing something entirely different until the block is reduced. In classrooms, we should reduce anxiety-producing situations that might cause students to develop writer's block, such as providing a variety of *prewriting* strategies; scheduling significant amounts of class time for *drafting;* encouraging students to talk through their ideas either with other students or with the teacher; limiting writing on demand assignments; allowing students to work on other classroom projects for a short while if writer's block is not alleviated by other strategies; and recognizing that writer's block causes anxiety in the writer and thus should be treated with sensitivity.

**writing process:**  The term used to describe the repeatable steps writers take when they write. It is, however, important to note that while we can generally categorize these steps into *prewriting, drafting, revising,* and *editing* stages, there is a significant element of idiosyncrasy in individual writers' application of these stages. Teachers should guide students through the stages but should not force students to go through each step in exactly the same manner. For example, outlining as a prewriting strategy might not work for all writers or for all writing tasks, so it might be counterproductive to require an outline before students can move into the drafting stage. An important aspect of the writing process is *recursiveness.*

**writing workshop:**  An approach to writing instruction characterized, in general, by the following practices: Students are permitted frequent and substantive writing periods when, ideally, they are working on self-selected writing tasks. Talk among students (about their writing, of course) is encouraged as a means of creating a social environment in which students share ideas about the process and the specific task. The teacher moves from behind the desk and interacts with students at all stages of the process. Students are encouraged to report frequently on the progress they are making toward completing their writing tasks. *Minilessons* take precedence over formal lectures so as to preserve writing time for students. At appropriate points in the workshop, students conference with the teacher and engage in peer editing sessions. For a thorough explanation of the writing workshop, including real examples from actual classrooms, you might want to read Atwell's *In the middle: New understandings about writing, reading, and learning* (1998).

# Classroom Practices: Writing

Writing is one of the most diverse areas of English language arts. When we teach writing, we work with everything from parts of speech to developing self-confidence in our student writers to technical aspects of manuscript preparation—all of which can be presented in the classroom in ways that alienate our student writers *or* that encourage their development into competent, confident writers. Thus, it is important to be familiar with some of the things we can do to make the teaching of writing a positive experience for our students. The list below presents only a few of the attitudes and practices that are conducive to creating a good teaching environment for writing.

- The teacher conveys excitement and/or enthusiasm about writing and the writing process.
- The teacher is honest about writing and the writing process. Students need to know that writing is frequently difficult and sometimes tedious but almost always quite rewarding.
- The teacher actively writes, to the extent possible, with students as they work through writing tasks. Among many other benefits, writing with your students will enable you to refine writing tasks and to discover "quirks" that might derail students' responses to the task. And, students love reading and commenting on texts that their teacher has produced.
- Writing can occur every day in a variety of contexts. In other words, "writing" doesn't have to be identified only with writing workshop or formal essay assignments.
- To the extent possible, the teacher utilizes writing workshop practices that encourage socialization among students, that promote self-awareness of writing practices among students, and that permit teacher intervention at appropriate points in the process.
- The teacher uses evaluation of writing to promote achievement in student writing competence.
- Teachers should make use of technological applications, such as word processing and Internet resources, to help students grow in their effectiveness as writers.

If you have had no methods courses in writing, you might want to read Chapter 2 of Zemelman and Daniels' *A community of writers: Teaching writing in the junior and senior high school* (1988) included in the Selected Resources in this chapter. The chapter includes a list of fifteen practices that characterize classrooms in which students demonstrate growth in writing (pp. 20–30) and that will give you a more detailed description of good teaching practices in writing.

## Other Areas of Writing Practice and Pedagogy

### Research

For each grade level (even the EC-4 levels), there is a TEKS writing category focused on research and inquiry, which suggests that questions on teaching research skills are likely to appear on the test. You should read through the

Writing/research/inquiry category of at least one TEKS grade level applicable to your certification level. Pay attention to the types of skills students are expected to have in this area and try to distance your own approach to research from the approach presented in TEKS. For example, in TEKS, research begins with formulation of research questions and use of prior knowledge to direct research. Your own experience may suggest that if you are tackling a research project, you may start out not knowing anything about the topic; consequently, it would be difficult to frame questions or use prior knowledge. You will have to assume that in a TEKS-perfect classroom, the teacher would help students implement inquiry activities and activate prior knowledge on any given topic.

Also note that use of technology is included in the research/inquiry TEKS categories. Assume this includes not only usual document preparation skills but also Internet and database research skills and multimedia technology skills for presenting the results of research. If you have minimal knowledge of newer research-related technologies, before you take your test, you should seek out a knowledgeable friend or institutional staff person (like a librarian or computer lab attendant) for tutoring in this area. You should also read some of the technology-related resources included in the Selected Resources section of Chapter 7.

Finally, you should know, at the minimum, what documentation of research results involves, including how to integrate source information into a student text without plagiarizing, how to cite sources in the text, how to cite Internet and other electronically accessed sources, and how to prepare a Works Cited or Reference page. Hult and Huckin (2002), cited in the Selected Resources for writing in this chapter, includes a multi-chapter section on research. If you feel less than confident about your ability to manage objective items related to teaching the research process, then you should look over the research section of the Hult and Huckin book. Don't be concerned about the fact that the book is aimed at a college freshman audience; you need to know the general processes, terminology, approaches, and text forms related to research; these will be the same regardless of the certification level you are working toward.

## Grammar Knowledge

The wording of TEKS and educator standards in the writing categories strongly suggests that grammar knowledge is an important aspect of TExES preparation. As you work through the sample test items in the TExES preparation manuals, you will notice that several items require knowledge of specific grammatical terms. Thus, your TExES preparation should include review of basic grammar terms and concepts. At the very least, you should refresh your knowledge of the following terms:

- Sentence types (simple, compound, complex, compound-complex)
- Clauses
- Phrases
- Verb forms
- Parts of speech

- Pronoun forms and usage
- Agreement rules
- Basic punctuation rules
- Fragments
- Run-ons
- Comma splices

Grammar and usage handbooks are good sources for information on grammar terms; even an outdated handbook will be a good source. In addition, several of the books included in the Selected Resources section of this chapter include glossaries of grammar terms: Weaver (1996), pp. 243-260; Calderonello, Martin, and Blair (2003), pp. 447-459; and Hult and Huckin (2002), pp. 878-893.

Do not make the mistake of thinking that you need only the level of grammar knowledge appropriate to the certification level you are preparing for. In other words, to teach at the EC-4 level, you need as sophisticated a level of grammar knowledge as you do for teaching high school English. You may not envision yourself telling a first grader that his or her writing needs to include more embedded structures to improve coherence, but you should be able to assess the growth of the child as a writer by identifying types of grammatical structures that are attempted. Thus, to teach writing at any level, a strong foundation in grammar is a necessity.

## Linguistics and Writing

Some of the TEKS expectations in the writing categories and educator standards in writing suggest that teachers should possess knowledge of specialized areas of linguistics, such as sociolinguistics and historical linguistics—although these terms do not actually occur in TEKS and educator standards. This linguistic knowledge includes, for example, helping students understand the influence of other languages and cultures on English spelling, guiding students in appreciating language varieties, and knowing when a discourse style is appropriate for a particular writing or speaking task. If you took a general linguistics course and you still have your textbook, you might want to look through the table of contents for chapter headings that reflect some of the TEKS and educator standards statements that deal with language change, discourse choices, and language development. If you have had no linguistics courses, you might want to read the designated chapters in Fromkin, Rodman, and Hyams (2003) suggested in the Selected Resources section of this chapter.

## Student Writing

It is possible you have made it through your teacher prep program without exposure to actual student writing. If that is the case for you, you should make every effort to examine samples of writing produced by students at your TExES level. So, if you are testing at the EC-4 level, for example, you should know what the writing of kindergarteners and first through fourth graders looks like. You do not want to go into your exam not knowing how children at your certification level write. It is likely that you will have test items that include passages from student writing. Your ability to answer such items correctly will depend, to a great extent, on your familiarity with the features of student writing at your certification level.

---

**TEST PREP TIP 9: KNOW HOW STUDENTS WRITE**    You don't want to be surprised by the style, quality, and general tenor of student writing samples that may be included on your TExES exam. So, before you face your actual test, familiarize yourself with the writing of children at your certification level. Surprises about student writing, particularly the writing of children, could cause you to respond incorrectly to some writing items.

---

What can you do to familiarize yourself with student writing? Here are a few suggestions:

- If you have a friend or contact in a local public school, try to get him or her to show you samples of student writing. Keep in mind: You do not have to grade the writing or comment on it in any way. You just want to know what the writing of children at your certification level looks like.
- If you have younger siblings or young relatives, you might be able to get samples of school writing from them. They might have a portfolio they produced for their language arts class, and leafing through such a document will greatly enrich your understanding of the characteristics of student writing.
- Many of the articles and books in the Suggested Resources section of this chapter include samples of student writing.

## Test Item Exercises

The exercises that follow will provide an opportunity for you to test your understanding of the terms, concepts, and principles presented in the glossary and in the teaching practices section of this chapter. Before you examine the items, you should go back to Test Prep Tip 6 to review strategies for identifying the correct response in objective items.

### EC-4 Practice Item: Writing

(1) A first-grade teacher wants to develop her students' ability to communicate clearly by recognizing and correctly applying conventions of written English. (2) Which of the following activities might best meet this objective?

A. Students journal-write every day and the teacher marks all the errors they make in their daily entries.

B. The teacher has a "Correction Corner" station set up where students correct errors on worksheets when they finish other projects throughout the day.

C. The teacher conducts a five-minute quickwrite each day during which students write as much as they can on the prompt for the day and then exchange papers with each other to identify and correct their partner's errors.

D. The teacher guides the whole class through a daily "Fix the Sentence" exercise in which students collaboratively apply punctuation and capitalization to a text of approximately 10 words.

*Analysis.*    Sentence 1 provides important information that will be vital in selecting the appropriate response: The students are first graders. As a test taker, you should immediately note that first graders are likely to still be in emergent stages of literacy and thus have limited understanding of print and writing. Sentence 2 includes a qualifier—"best"—which should signal to you that all of the responses *could* meet the objective, but you need to use your knowledge of the level of the students and writing theory and pedagogy in general to select the most appropriate response.

- Response A: The most important clue in this response is the fact that students are writing journals. Journal writing should be nonthreatening. First graders are likely to have limited print awareness and will produce numerous invented spellings that only they themselves will be able to interpret. Thus, marking the errors in daily journals is likely to inhibit writing fluency.

- Response B: This activity focuses on errors in worksheets, an approach that discourages active learning and focuses attention on error rather than on effective application of conventions.

- Response C: The quickwrite activity might provide an opportunity for students to concentrate on quantity and thus could be used effectively to encourage idea development. However, exchanging papers to identify errors would be nonproductive at this grade level since many students would still be producing a large number of invented and phonetic spellings. This activity would introduce spelling as an issue when the teacher's objective is correct application of conventions of written English.

- Response D: This collaborative activity offers the best strategy for meeting the teacher's objective to help students correctly apply *conventions* of written English. Furthermore, the social setting encourages discussion among students about the rationale for applying capitalization and punctuation.

Response D is the best response.

## 4-8 Practice Item: Writing

(1) A middle school English teacher and a social studies teacher are team-teaching a four-week research unit for their sixth graders. (2) Working in groups, they will be researching and writing on the death penalty. (3) Which of the following activities would be the best beginning activity for this unit?

A. Watching excerpts from several movies (such as *The Green Mile, Dead Man Walking, The Chamber*) that deal with inmates on death row.
B. Working in groups to come up with questions about the death penalty that they can use to guide their initial research activities.
C. Having the students brainstorm in groups their feelings about the death penalty.
D. Having the school librarian give the class a presentation on common mistakes students make while conducting research.

*Analysis.*    Sentences 1 and 2 of the stem narrow this item to a research activity. This is an important concern since from the early grades, there is a separate TEKS category for writing/inquiry/research. (If you do not recall the general expectations in that TEKS category, review it right now.) As you read through the exercise, you need to make sure that the response you select reflects student expectations for that TEKS category. Sentence 3 includes an important qualifier: You are to select the best *beginning* activity for the research unit.

- Response A: Your first reaction to this response should be that it is a media literacy activity rather than a writing/research activity. Watching movie treatments of the death penalty would be more appropriate for a reflective or expressive purpose. Research requires examining legitimate sources on a designated topic. Perhaps later in the research process, students would benefit from this media literacy activity.
- Response B: While it might seem that students need initial guidance and/or externally provided information early in the research process, having students frame questions for research early in the process is actually the approach suggested by TEKS.
- Response C: Brainstorming to come up with *feelings* about the death penalty would be more appropriate for a reflective or expressive paper or perhaps even for a persuasive essay. In a research project, the writer's feelings might interfere with his or her ability to evaluate the legitimacy of research sources.
- Response D: The school librarian will be a valuable resource during the research process, but the focus of a librarian's presentation should be positive: In other words, students should be guided in what to do during the research process rather than warned about mistakes that they might make. In addition, such a presentation would be more valuable after students have made initial ventures into the research process.

Response B best fits the specifications of the stem.

## 8-12 Practice Item: Writing

(1) Ms. Chavez is working with her English III students in individual conferences to improve their style in their latest essay drafts. (2) The following passage is the opening paragraph to one student's essay.

Many people that go to college usually don't make it out. Students face a completely different world than the one they did in high school. It is a world of independence, responsibilities, and stress. It is a world they are not used to. Few students choose to adapt to the new environment and many of them would rather not face the situation. Some students have no choice but to drop out of college due to financial problems or maybe they have a job and are not able to manage their time between school and work.

(3) Which of the following comments should Ms. Chavez make in order to help this student improve the style of this paragraph?

  A. "Notice that all of the sentences begin with the noun or pronoun subject; perhaps you can rewrite some of the sentences to create some variety in sentence structure."
  B. "There are at least two comma faults in this paragraph. You need to correct those before you turn in the essay."
  C. "There are too many ideas with which most readers would disagree; you need to be more aware of your audience."
  D. "If the last sentence is the thesis of your essay, you need to revise it so that it is focused on only one problem."

*Analysis.* In any test item that includes an embedded passage, you must make sure you read the passage carefully. Sentence 1 specifies that the teacher is focused on one aspect of writing—style—during this student-teacher conference. You should also immediately make a mental note that style is a very specific aspect of writing involving mostly sentence structure and word choice. The level of the students—English III—is also important; TEKS expectations for junior students are higher than for grades 8, 9, or 10. Sentence 2 narrows the item to a specific paragraph; we do not know what is in the rest of the essay. Sentence 3 specifies that Ms. Chavez is conducting a directed teaching activity in which she makes specific suggestions rather than an independent learning activity in which the learner makes most of the decisions.

  ■ Response A: Careful reading of this passage should lead to the observation that although this writer has included a mixture of simple, compound, and complex sentences in this paragraph, the basic syntax of the sentences is the same: subject-verb-object order, which creates a simplistic style.
  ■ Response B: While correcting the comma errors would address the grammatical aspects of the passage, inserting commas where needed will not affect the style of the passage.
  ■ Response C: If the passage does in fact contain too many ideas, this is a coherence or unity problem not a stylistic problem.
  ■ Response D: Revising the thesis for focus is a unity issue not a stylistic concern.

Response A best meets the specifications of the item stem.

# Responding to Writing Items on Sample TExES Tests

Once you work through the reflections in this chapter, examine the glossary items, and read some of the books, chapters, and articles included in the Selected Resources, you should attempt the sample test items on writing in your TExES Preparation Manual. Remember that the analytical strategies you use (Test Prep Tip 6) are your best resource for getting ready for the actual test. So, try not to glance at the correct response in the answer key until you have worked through each writing item using the approach presented in the Test Exercises section above.

---

REFLECTION FOR YOUR TExES JOURNAL:   How do you assess your level of preparation for the writing pedagogy segment of your TExES exam? Do you feel there are areas in which you are particularly strong or somewhat weak? How do you plan to address the weaknesses you detect in your preparation for the writing pedagogy items?

---

## Chapter Summary

- Reflect on your own writing process as you study the terms and concepts related to the writing portion of TExES. Thinking about how you write will give you a context for many of the terms, concepts, and practices included in the writing components of your study materials.
- Take advantage of the Selected Resources to review or to fill in gaps in your writing practice and pedagogy knowledge.
- Familiarize yourself with the writing of students at your certification level.

## Selected Resources: Writing Practice and Pedagogy

Atwell, N. (1998). *In the middle: New understandings about writing, reading, and learning* (2nd ed.). Portsmouth, NH: Heinemann.

This book provides a comprehensive, practice-based discussion/demonstration of the writing workshop. If you do not have time to read the whole book, focus on Section II: Writing and Reading Workshop. Any fuzziness you may feel about how the writing workshop functions in a classroom will be eliminated once you read this section. In addition, you will recognize many terms and concept from TEKS, which Atwell defines by example. While based on Atwell's experiences with middle schoolers, the concepts and practices are applicable to all certification levels.

Behymer, A. (2003). Kindergarten writing workshop. *The Reading Teacher, 57*(1), 85-88.

Behymer offers practical applications of the writing workshop in a kindergarten environment. The EC-4 TExES candidate will find in this article many TEKS-relevant terms and concepts, presented in the context of teaching scenarios.

Calderonello, A., Martin, V. S., & Blair, K. L. (2003). *Grammar for language arts teachers.* New York: Longman.

If you feel insecure about your knowledge of basic grammar, this book will give you confidence as you approach your TExES exam. The authors provide a comprehensive overview of basic terms and concepts needed to teach writing effectively. Not only are terms defined and illustrated, but in many instances, the authors also explain the significance of certain types of grammar problems in the context of teaching writing. The book is quite user-friendly, with chapter overviews and boldface terms that allow the TExES candidate to quickly locate terms and definitions.

Calkins, L. M. (1994). *The art of teaching writing* (new edition). Portsmouth, NH: Heinemann.

The most valuable aspect of this book is the analysis of children's writing by grade levels. EC-4 certification candidates will find this book illuminating because of the numerous samples of student writing provided. Calkins analyzes the features of children's writing at each grade level. The other sections of the book deal with implementation of the writing workshop and cover many areas addressed by TEKS and educator standards, including assessment, writing in different genres, and connecting school and home in literacy development.

Fromkin, V., Rodman, R., & Hyams, N. (2003). *An introduction to language* (7th ed.). Boston: Wadsworth.

Three chapters in this book are valuable resources for the TExES candidate who needs to review or learn anew concepts about language and their impact on writing pedagogy. Chapter 1, What Is Language; Chapter 10, Language and Society; and Chapter 11, Language Change: The Syllables of Time.

Hult, C. A., & Huckin, T. H. (2002). *New century handbook* (2nd ed.). New York: Longman.

This is an excellent resource for the TExES candidate who wants to know the sorts of topics that constitute writing instruction. Although aimed at a college freshman audience, the content is applicable to all levels of writing instruction. For example, a TExES candidate who might be unsure about what constitutes unity in writing could read the chapter on structuring paragraphs. Also particularly applicable for TExES preparation is the discussion of technology and writing, including topics like desktop publishing, Web page design, and word processing. Two glossaries, one on computer terms and one on grammar terms, are also useful for clarifying terms and topics applicable to TExES preparation in the area of writing pedagogy and practice.

McGee, L. M., & Richgels, D. J. (2004). *Literacy's beginnings: Supporting young readers and writers* (4th ed.). Boston: Allyn and Bacon.

Although no separate chapters on acquisition of writing skills and competencies occur in this book, the TExES candidate will find valuable information about the writing development of preschool to grade 3 children. Particularly useful features of this book are the key concepts lists at the beginning of each chapter, the abundant examples of children's writing, and boldfacing of important terms. Terms and concepts that occur in TEKS and educator standards also occur in this book in the context of actual literacy development scenarios.

Rief, L. (2003). *Writing matters.* Voices from the Middle, 11(2), 8-12.

Student writing samples and situations make up most of Rief's article, but the TExES candidate will find in her discussion of student writing important applications of TEKS-relevant terms. In addition, Rief uses the student writing samples to compose a list of good teaching practices for writing; these practices enable the TExES candidate to understand how student expectations presented in TEKS and teacher expectations presented in educator standards can be manifested in actual teaching situations.

Soven, M. I. (1999). *Teaching writing in middle and secondary schools.* Boston: Allyn and Bacon.

This text provides a good mix of theory and pedagogy: It presents issues, concerns, and controversies in the teaching of writing while also explaining the rationale behind good teaching practices. In addition, you will encounter terms and concepts that reflect TEKS and educator standards. Although aimed at a secondary teaching audience, this book is a valuable resource for all certification levels. Two chapters are particularly applicable for TExES preparation: Chapter 3, Teaching the Writing Process, and Chapter 5, Teaching about Sentences. Finally, Soven includes numerous samples of student writing throughout her text.

Street, C. (2000). Using word-processing software to improve the writing attitudes of reluctant writers. *English in Texas, 30*(2), 35-37.

Street describes the writing workshop in a computer lab setting. TExES candidates who have thought about the way word processing tools enhance their own writing process will learn from this article how to translate that experience into good teaching practices. Street focuses on "reluctant" writers—by his definition, students who resist revision—but his advice applies to all levels and types of writers. Important TEKS-relevant terms, particularly those that apply to incorporating technology into the teaching of writing, appear throughout the article.

Weaver, C. (1996). *Teaching grammar in context.* Portsmouth, NH: Heinemann.

The TExES candidate who thinks of teaching grammar as something that happens via worksheets will find this book illuminating. Weaver clearly explains how and why grammar should be taught in the context of teaching the writing process. Numerous student writing samples are used throughout the book to illustrate students' competencies in grammar at various grade levels. Figure 5.13 (pp. 142-144) offers her suggestions for aspects of grammar that should be taught from kindergarten through college; the TExES candidate can use this component of Weaver's book to clarify terminology in TEKS and educator standards. Also quite helpful for a certification candidate is Weaver's Glossary of Grammatical Terms (pp. 243-260).

Zemelman, S., & Daniels, H. (1988). *A community of writers: Teaching writing in the junior and senior high school.* Portsmouth, NH: Heinemann.

Despite its apparent "datedness," this is one of the most thorough resources for preparing to teach writing in secondary schools. The authors balance theoretical presentation with practical applications. One of the most valuable aspects of the book is the authors' theory-grounded explanations of why we do what we do in best practice writing classrooms. Any TExES candidate who does not understand the difference between the process and the product approaches to teaching writing should study the chart on pp. 18-19. Chapter 18, Integrated Activities for Learning Subject Matter, includes illustrative units for using writing in content area classes.

# CHAPTER

# 4 Literature

If you are a typical English education student, most of your discipline-related teacher prep courses have probably been in literature. So, you probably can analyze literary texts, place literary excerpts in the appropriate literary period, compare features of literary texts, connect literary texts to social and historical contexts, and discuss the impact of literary devices on our appreciation of literature. However, the appreciation of literature and the skills required to read literary texts represent only part of the knowledge you need to successfully respond to the literature items on the TExES exam you attempt. A significant portion of the literature items on TExES exams will test your ability to *teach* literature. This chapter is designed to help you coordinate your knowledge of literature with your knowledge of pedagogical strategies and approaches appropriate to teaching literature in K–12 classrooms. If you are testing at the 8–12 level, you will also be required to write a short essay as part of your test. This chapter includes a section on how to prepare for the essay and a sample essay that is annotated to call your attention to things you should include in the essay.

## Teaching Literature: An Overview

Let's start our literature study with a definition of the term as we'll use it in TExES preparation. We risk oversimplification in providing a definition, but we need to establish boundaries for our discussion.

LITERATURE: A WORKING DEFINITION    Literature refers to the body of texts that are imaginative in nature although usually meant to illustrate or comment on significant issues that affect us all. Literary texts, in the context of TExES preparation, should be distinguished from nonfiction texts, which are considered, for the most part, to be factually as opposed to imaginatively constructed. An important aspect of literature is aesthetics, so that the "message" or story conveyed must be decoded by recognizing, understanding, and appreciating the literary elements and devices the author uses in constructing the text. Literary texts are usually divided into the major genres of poetry, fiction, and drama.

The teaching of literature changes significantly as we move through progressively higher grade levels. In the early grades, it is difficult to separate literature from general literacy instruction. EC-4 teachers are charged with teaching young readers fundamental aspects about reading literature, things like the concept of story, the difference between fiction and nonfiction, story grammar, and application of general reading principles to the special texts that we recognize as literature. TEKS and educator standards for middle school and high school ELA suggest that much of what goes on in those grades continues to be fundamental training in how to read literature, how to recognize different types of literary texts, how to relate literary texts to other texts, how to differentiate literary texts from other texts, and how to talk about and analyze literary texts using the terminology appropriate to literature. At all certification levels, the ability to teach literature assumes extensive knowledge of a wide repertoire of literary texts appropriate for that level. In addition, TEKS and educator standards at all certification levels point out the importance of cultural awareness in the context of literary study.

---

**REFLECTION FOR YOUR TExES JOURNAL:**   Think a bit about your experiences with literature. What is your favorite poem, novel, story, or play? What is the major appeal of that favorite text? In what ways have your teachers helped you appreciate literature?

---

## Coordinating TEKS, Educator Standards, and Test Competencies in Literature

Figure 4.1 shows you how to coordinate TEKS, educator standards, test competencies, and course work in literature. You should note that there are no distinct TEKS categories for literature; instead, the literature-related TEKS are embedded in the following *reading* TEKS categories: reading/literary response, reading/text structures/literary concepts, and reading/culture.

---

**A NOTE FOR EC-4 AND 4-8 CANDIDATES:**   If you are an EC-4 candidate, please note that there are no educator standards exclusively devoted to literature; instead, references to children's literature, literary genres, and literary elements occur in specific knowledge and skills statements for the standards and competencies listed in the chart. For example, EC-4 Standard VII is labeled Reading Comprehension. The expanded description of that standard includes several statements—7.10s and 7.11s—that charge the teacher with facilitating and encouraging students' response to literature and with teaching elements of literature (SBEC, 2002c). Similarly, there are no 4-8 standards exclusively devoted to literature, but there are knowledge and skills statements that address the middle school teacher's knowledge of a wide range of literature, ability to help students respond to children's and young adult literature, and other competencies.

If you are an EC-4 or 4-8 candidate, read carefully through the educator standards and test competencies identified in the Literature Study Chart to locate the knowledge and skills statements that apply specifically to literature knowledge and pedagogy. Look for terms such as "literary genres," "wide range of literature," "children's literature," "stories," "literary analysis."

Let's designate green as our color code for literature materials. Take time now to highlight TEKS literature categories, literature educator standards, and literature

**FIGURE 4.1   Literature Study Chart**

| EC-4 | | | |
|---|---|---|---|
| **TEKS K-4** | **Educator Standards** | **Test Competencies** | **Courses** |
| Reading/literary response Reading/text structures/ literary concepts Reading/culture | Standard IV. Literacy Development and Practice Standard VII. Reading Comprehension | Competency 004 (Literacy Development) Competency 007 (Reading Comprehension) | Sophomore lit Lit survey courses Specialized lit courses (poetry, author-based, novel, special topics, etc.) Children's lit Reading Literacy development |

| 4-8 | | | |
|---|---|---|---|
| **TEKS Grades 4 & 5 TEKS Middle School** | **Educator Standards** | **Competencies** | **Courses** |
| Reading/literary response Reading/text structures/ literary concepts Reading/culture | Standard II. Foundations of Reading Standard IV. Reading Comprehension | Competency 005 (Reading Applications) | Sophomore lit Lit survey courses Specialized lit courses (poetry, author-based, novel, special topics, etc.) Children's lit Adolescent lit Reading Literacy development |

| 8-12 | | | |
|---|---|---|---|
| **TEKS Grade 8 TEKS High School** | **Educator Standards** | **Competencies** | **Courses** |
| Reading/literary response Reading/text structures/ literary concepts Reading/culture | Standard IV | Competency 006 Competency 007 | Sophomore lit Lit survey courses Specialized lit courses (poetry, author-based, novel, special topics, etc.) Children's lit Adolescent lit Reading Literacy development |

test competencies in green for easy reference. Other materials that will aid in your TExES literature study include

- Textbooks from literature and literacy development courses
- Literature anthologies, novels, children's books, young adult novels, poetry collections, plays
- Supplementary texts such as handbooks to literature
- Textbooks from reading courses (many have chapters devoted to teaching literature)
- Class notes, handouts, essays, and tests

---

**REFLECTION FOR YOUR TExES JOURNAL:**   Read through the TEKS, educator standards, and test competencies for literature. Make a list of key terms, marking terms that you are unsure about. What questions do you have about literature content and pedagogy after reading through TEKS, standards, and competencies?

---

# A Glossary of Selected Literature Terms and Concepts

Many of the terms explained in this glossary are applicable to all aspects of *reading* (see Chapter 2), but for the purpose of studying for the literature component of the test, we are focusing on how these terms apply specifically to the teaching of literature.

**character:**   One of the literary terms that enables students to talk about literature. Students must be led to see how realistic characters can be even though they are imaginative constructions in a text. As levels of comprehension develop, students must explore character motivation, recognize that characters' actions have consequences that impact the outcome of the story, and find connections (similarities and differences) among characters in a variety of literary texts. An important aspect of children's literacy development is recognizing that characters can seem real because conflicts and situations presented in literature are similar to circumstances of real life. As readers mature, they should be led to see differences in character types, such as round and flat characters, protagonists and antagonists, and stock characters.

**character cluster:**   A *graphic organizer* intended to help students understand a character's features and/or motivations. The character cluster is an adaptation of a *semantic map* or a *web* to the context of literature study. The character's name is placed at the center of the web with the character's traits attached to it. This is a good strategy for helping readers move from literal comprehension of a character to interpretative and critical comprehension that leads to a more in-depth understanding of a character. Character clusters can be created by individual students or by groups depending on how the teacher wants to use the clusters.

**character journal:**   A strategy for helping students understand characters in literature. Students write a journal in the role of a character from a literary work they are reading. The point of this activity is to help students engage with characters and to understand the motivations that drive the character to act as he or she does in the literary work.

**community of readers:**   The sense of togetherness created when the teacher and students work together to achieve comprehension of a literary text. In a community of readers, questions are welcomed, discussion is encouraged, respect for multiple readings of a text is fostered, and authority about the meaning of a text is shared by all readers, rather than claimed by the teacher alone.

**construction of meaning:**   The concept that meaning in a literary text must be created by the reader as he or she interacts with the text and with other readers. Thus, discussions of literary texts must involve socialization with other readers, invite multiple responses to a text, and be accepting of nontraditional readings of the text.

**creative dramatics:**   A type of student response to literature. Students may act out or perform aspects of a literary text demonstrating their understanding of events, character motivation, conflict in the plot, and other elements. Creative dramatics offers a teacher multiple levels of applications: cooperative learning, oral language, assessment of comprehension, and reader response.

**culture:**   The ways of life, customs, and beliefs valued by members of specialized communities, foreign countries, and ethnic groups. A good bit of literature includes depictions of specific cultures. Students are expected to understand that literature enables readers to learn about and understand cultures different from their own. So, we could talk about the "culture of the South" presented in William Faulkner's *The Sound and the Fury,* the insights into Jewish family and community life presented in Chaim Potok's *The Chosen,* the revelations about Native American beliefs and family life presented in Tomie De Paola's *The Legend of the Bluebonnet.* Students should also be encouraged to find connections between their own culture and the cultures they encounter in literary texts.

**fiction/nonfiction distinction:**   A distinction that teachers must guide young readers to understand, particularly as they are first acquiring literacy. Teaching story grammar and the concept of story is an important part of showing readers that nonfiction is based on fact or interpretations of real events, while fiction is created from the imagination even though it may represent real-world events, times, and people.

**film versions of literary texts:**   A resource for helping students understand literature. Film versions of novels and stories can be used in a variety of ways in the classroom. Sometimes films help students construct meaning from a text that might be challenging (this is why so many teachers rely on film versions of Shakespeare's plays to help students connect the language of the play with the action and drama that the characters are experiencing). Films also help students visualize elements of text, particularly if they are unfamiliar with the era or location in which the text is set. Students must be taught that films are different versions of the literary text, that they cannot substitute for reading literary texts, and that a film is a type of text that requires *media literacy* skills for understanding (see Chapter 6).

**Freytag's pyramid:**   A triangle used to illustrate the structure of literature. Usually rising action is represented on the left side of the triangle, rising toward the climax (the apex of the triangle), with falling action forming the right side of the triangle.

**genres:**   Forms or types of literary texts that have distinguishing characteristics, such as poems, stories, novels, and plays. Each of these broad genres can be subdivided in to even more specific forms with quite distinctive features. For example, within the genre of poetry, there are sonnets, epic poems, lyric poems, sestinas, limericks, and many other specific poetic forms.

**graphic organizers:**   Character clusters, story trees, story boards, plot maps, and other devices intended to help students understand story structure and characters. The graphic organizer enables students to visualize connections among different aspects of the story elements, or, as in the case of a character cluster, to focus on one specific aspect of the story.

**illustrations:**   Art, pictures, and other graphics that authors and editors use to enhance and/or complement the reader's appreciation and understanding of a written text. Young readers need to learn that in picture books, where text is limited, illustrations are vital to their understanding of the story, so they need to be taught how to "read" the illustrations and integrate the information provided by illustrations into the text.

**literary devices:**   Figures of speech (e.g., metaphor, simile, synecdoche, metonomy, apostrophe) and strategies (such as irony, symbolism, suspense, foreshadowing) used by authors to enrich a reader's appreciation of a literary text. Students must understand that literary devices allow authors to use language artistically rather than informatively. In other words, literary devices call for departure from the ordinary and accepted uses of language in order to create the "poetic" or artistic quality of literature. Students must be taught that literary devices cannot be read only at the *literal* level; understanding literary devices occurs through *inferential* and *evaluative* comprehension.

**literary forms:**   More or less the same thing as "genres." However, in the early grade TEKS, the term is also used to differentiate between literary texts and nonfiction texts, oral performances, and nonprint media. Many of the TEKS reading/text structures/literary concepts statements include lists of literary forms. As a test taker, you should make sure you are able to identify the distinguishing features of these forms.

**literary terms:**   The vocabulary students should acquire in order to discuss and analyze literature. At the early reading stages, literary terms include *author, illustrator, story problem, character, setting, plot, events.* As readers become more sophisticated, more literary terms must be added to their repertoire of terms. Specific terms mentioned in TEKS include *antagonist, protagonist, structure in poetry, epic, ballad, comic relief, playwright, scene, dialogue, stage.* Test candidates should see these as examples of the types of terms that might show up on objective items on the TExES.

**literature circles:**   A strategy for helping students talk about books. Literature circles to some extent mimic book clubs in which members select the book they want to read and then spend time discussing it and responding to it. So, literature circles in the classroom can be based on student-selected books; however, the books may also be chosen from a list selected by the teacher. Literature circles can also be used to foster student engagement in a novel that the whole class is reading. Although the teacher must initially guide students in structuring and setting up literature circles, eventually teacher intervention in literature circles should be reduced in order to allow students to learn how to comment about books and how to respond to others' ideas. (See definition of *literature circles* in Chapter 2 as well.)

**plot:**   The events, conflicts, and actions that lead to the outcome of the story. In a literary text, these elements are tightly controlled by the author to ensure that the reader understands the theme or message of the text. In early reading stages, readers may be able to discuss plot only at the literal level. *Story grammar* can be used to help young readers recognize and understand the various elements of plot.

**prereading:**   A brief activity designed to stimulate student interest in a literary text they are about to read. This must occur before the text is read. It may make use of prior knowledge about an element of the text; it may present a thematic element of the text through a nonprint medium; or it may involve props designed to get students talking about some aspect of the text. (See definition of *prereading* in Chapter 2.)

**reader response:**   An approach to teaching literature that encourages students to respond to elements of a literary work personally and individually. The fundamental tenet of this approach is that readers construct meaning by interacting with a text personally and meaningfully in contrast to extracting meaning that exists absolutely and consistently in the text. A reader response classroom encourages students to engage in social interaction as they listen to each other's responses to the text and as they use other students' responses to construct their own understanding and appreciation of the text.

**reader response journal:**   A highly productive activity for eliciting student responses to literary texts. In its simplest form, a reader response journal includes short excerpts (usually just a sentence or so) chosen by the reader from an assigned literary text to which writers respond by writing about how or why the passage impacted them, a connection they see between themselves and the story, or questions raised by the passage. Reader response journals are aimed at helping students engage with a text and at providing a basis for student-centered class discussion. Instead of conducting a teacher-directed discussion with questions about the assigned reading, the teacher can ask students to share their reader response journal entries. In other versions of the reader response journal, students can respond in writing to each other's reader responses. Other terms for this activity include *response journal, dialogic* *journal*, or *response log*. Reader response journals can also be integrated into *literature circles* as a means of preparing students to actively participate in discussion.

**relevance of literature to students' own lives:** An important pedagogical attitude supported by TEKS, educator standards, and current pedagogical theories. To respond meaningfully to literature, students should be guided to find connections between literary texts and their own lives. Because students do not "extract" meaning from literary texts as they do from nonfiction texts that might be read to gain information or knowledge, we need to foster a classroom atmosphere in which we help students find relevance in the literature we assign and discuss in class. This approach is important even for older students. We should not expect students of any age to be inherently interested in the literary texts we teach.

**response to literary texts:** Reactions and reflections about literature. Teachers must be able to elicit a variety of student responses to literary texts through talking, questioning, speculating, writing, connecting music and/or art to a text, or creating graphic displays that reflect the text. An important element of response is the connection between the literary text and students' own lives.

**storyboard:** A visual representation of story elements, such as plot, setting, conflict, resolution. The student draws pictures, usually in a grid, that indicate his or her comprehension of the story elements. This strategy is usually appropriated in helping emerging readers understand the concept of story. The storyboard can be a collaborative effort in small groups or a whole class environment, or it can be produced by individual readers. In either case, it provides the teacher a means of assessing the children's ability to understand basic story elements.

**story grammar:** The underlying "rules" that enable readers to recognize a story as a story, differentiating it from a nonfiction text. Guiding students to understand story grammar is an important aspect of the EC-4 teacher's literacy instruction. Young readers must be taught to identify the setting, recognize the event that triggers the story problem, articulate the problem that creates the conflict, and recognize the outcome that results from characters' actions. For young readers, story grammar may be taught using a graphic organizer in which students fill in actual sentences or parts of sentences from a story to demonstrate their understanding of the components of story grammar.

**story schema:** The set of expectations that readers have as they encounter a literary narrative and that enables them to read and appreciate one literary text after another. These expectations include, for example, the understanding that stories have a plot, that some event early in the story triggers story problems, that characters respond to these problems and influence the outcome of the story, and that suspense and other literary elements contribute to the reader's appreciation of the story. Story schema must also include the reader's understanding that although literary texts are creative constructions, they may be based on real-world events reconstructed through the author's imagination.

**story structure:** The understanding of what constitutes a "story." This knowledge includes being able to distinguish a literary text from a nonfiction text. *Simple* story structure includes the understanding that stories include events that trigger a problem, that characters react to that problem, and that the story ends when there is a resolution to that problem. For emergent readers, understanding of story structure may be supported with oral story telling. While historical, scientific, and current events can in fact be represented as narratives (e.g., the "story" of Paul Revere, the "story" of Betsy Ross, the "story" of Frederick Douglass), in the context of TExES materials, *story structure* primarily refers to literary texts in which setting, character motivation, complicating events, and story outcome are manipulated by an author as part of a creative, imaginative text.

**text structures:** The pattern that readers expect in stories. Young readers can be taught to use story grammar to construct meaning of literary texts. As readers mature, they can use the formal literary terms (e.g., rising action, conflict, climax) to construct the meaning of the text.

**thematic units:** An approach to teaching literature that focuses on a theme illustrated across a variety of genres and/or disciplines. Themes should be relevant to students' lives and interests, and teachers should use recommended pedagogical strategies to help students see connections between thematic topics and their own lives. Common thematic topics include friendship, dealing with authority, family relationships, peer pressure, fitting in with the crowd, maintaining independence, decision making, and facing obstacles.

**theme:** The general, abstract statement about life, the world, or humanity that a literary text offers. Students should understand that all literary texts deal with issues, and the outcome of a story helps us construct the story theme. Students should also understand that a single theme can apply to multiple texts across a variety of reading levels and genres. For example, the theme "Perseverance leads to the accomplishment of one's goals" can apply to Eudora Welty's "A Worn Path" as well as to the children's story *The Little Engine That Could*, although for younger students the theme likely would be stated more simply, perhaps as "If you want to reach a goal, you shouldn't give up." Students should be taught that a theme is constructed by the reader on the basis of events, characters' actions, outcomes, and conflicts in stories and novels.

**young adult literature:** Literary texts specifically aimed at an adolescent audience. Usually a literary work is considered "young adult literature" if it features a teenager or preadolescent as the protagonist, focuses on events and issues relevant to adolescents, and utilizes language, style, and text structures aimed at the target audience. While many traditionally taught novels feature adolescents as protagonists—such as William Golding's *Lord of the Flies* (1959) or Rudolfo Anaya's *Bless Me, Ultima* (1972)—most books categorized as "young adult novels" are specifically written for young people rather than a general audience. And, young adult novels do not provide the reflective, adult comments offered by older narrators writing about their adolescence. In a young adult novel, the point of view is generally non-reflective; the reader knows no more about the situation than the protagonist. If you have never read a young adult novel, prior to taking your TExES, you should read a few novels by well-known young adult novelists such as Madeleine L'Engle, Robert Cormier, Avi, and S. E. Hinton so that you can compare young adult novels to traditional novels that happen to have young people as protagonists.

# Classroom Practices: Literature

Knowing some best teaching practices for literature will be helpful in figuring out correct responses to literature pedagogy items on the actual TExES test. The following practices are suggested by TEKS, standards, and competencies, but they also represent the approaches advocated by current books and articles devoted to teaching literature.

- ELA teachers should present the study of literature as an enjoyable experience. This involves helping students find connections between literary texts and their own lives and treating literary texts as works of art that can be examined aesthetically and analytically rather than as texts from which information must be extracted.

- ELA teachers demonstrate to students their own love of literature through activities such as reading to students short passages from books they themselves are currently reading and talking about their own experiences as students of literature.

- ELA teachers demonstrate familiarity with a wide range of literary texts, including traditional works from world, British, and American literature; contemporary literature; ethnic literature; young adult literature; and children's literature. This breadth of literary knowledge enables the teacher to move beyond traditional canonical texts and enrich students' understanding of other cultures as they are presented through literature. In addition, the teacher will be able to help students make choices about literature they chose to read.

- ELA teachers create a community of readers in which student comments about the meaning of literary texts are encouraged and in which the teacher fosters an atmosphere of trust, respect, and open-mindedness regarding discussion of literary texts.
- ELA teachers select activities, create a class environment, and cultivate attitudes that help students become lifelong readers of literature.
- ELA teachers guide students toward the understanding that meaning in literary texts is constructed by personal involvement with the text and through social interaction with other readers.

REFLECTION FOR YOUR TExES JOURNAL: What are some of the most enjoyable or enriching experiences you've had in your literature classes? In other words, what specific strategies have your language arts teachers and literature professors incorporated to enhance your appreciation of literature?

# Test Item Exercises

The practice items are intended to show you how you can draw on all the elements discussed in this chapter as you read through test questions to determine the correct response to *pedagogy* items. It is important to note that while specific literary works may be mentioned in these pedagogy items, actual knowledge of those literary works is usually not relevant to the item. The pedagogy items test your ability to teach specific aspects of literature, like theme or characterization. If a literary work is mentioned in pedagogy items, it is simply to set a realistic scenario. Finally, as you read through the practice items, keep in mind that on the 8-12 test, you will also face objective items that test your knowledge of the *content* of literature. We will address that aspect of the test later in the chapter.

## EC-4 Practice Item: Literature

(1) A language arts teacher is using a big book to read *The True Story of the Three Little Pigs* (Scieszka, 1989) to her first graders, a retelling of the traditional children's three little pigs story from the point of view of the wolf who claims he was "framed." (2) The teacher wants to develop the students' ability to understand character motivation in a story. (3) Which of the following activities might best accomplish this goal?

A. After the children listen to and follow the story in the big book, the teacher asks the children to draw pictures presenting the main events in the story.

B. The teacher leads a class discussion in which she asks students to talk about times when they have been misunderstood.
C. Working in small groups, the children develop a character cluster showing the main character's traits.
D. The teacher has students work in groups to produce a collage of magazine pictures that remind them of the story events.

*Analysis.*   In EC-4 items, the age of the learner is of vital importance since literacy levels determine what the child is able to do at that point. This stem specifies that the learners are first graders. This should indicate to you that the children are likely to still be at the literal level of comprehension and to still be acquiring story grammar. The item, you should note, focuses on character motivation, which should be an indication that the teacher is trying to move her students into the inferential level of comprehension.

- Response A: Drawing in response to a story is a relatively common activity to assign to children at this age. It is a good strategy for reinforcing story grammar since the pictures will indicate what the children understand about the story. In fact, the response specifies that the children's drawings are to represent main events in the story, which is more likely to reinforce the understanding of sequence of events (literal comprehension) rather than character motivation (inferential comprehension).
- Response B: This class discussion activity seems designed to help the children relate to the theme and the events of the story. While it is a productive socialization activity, it does not focus on character motivation.
- Response C: Character clusters, a type of graphic organizer, can be productively used to help readers of all ages identify and analyze the individual qualities a character displays in a story. Identifying character traits is a good first step to discussing why a character acts as he or she does in a narrative. Because character traits are usually *inferred* from character's actions, dialogue, or exposition, this activity moves readers beyond literal comprehension toward inferential comprehension.
- Response D: Creating a collage from magazine cut-outs is a good activity for promoting students' understanding that story events are relevant to the "real" world. The activity also promotes social interaction that is likely to contribute to the children's understanding of the story. However, this response does not specifically focus on character motivation; instead the response specifies that students use the collage to represent story events.

Response C best meets the specifications of the item stem.

## 4-8 Practice Item: Literature

(1) Students in a middle school English classroom are reading Sharon Creech's *Walk Two Moons* (1994). (2) The teacher wants to ensure that students read their daily chapter assignments and understand the events and the characters' actions. (3) Which of the following assignments would best meet this goal?

A. The teacher assigns a literature journal, encouraging students to make at least one entry for each chapter.
B. At the beginning of each class meeting, the teacher asks students if they have any questions about the chapters they read.
C. The teacher administers a 10-item objective quiz each class period prior to beginning discussion of the assignment.
D. The teacher asks students to bring a newspaper clipping to class each day that is relevant to the events in the chapters assigned for that day.

*Analysis.* This item focuses on a common problem in extended literature assignments: getting students to do their daily reading assignments without turning the reading activity into a classroom chore that does not promote literacy development. That the teacher is interested in monitoring the students' understanding of the events and characters' actions indicates that he or she is focusing on *assessing* the students' comprehension.

- Response A: Literature journals are both student-centered and assessment-oriented. Requiring one entry for each chapter encourages students to read actively and it provides the teacher an authentic means of assessing the students' comprehension of characters' actions and events.
- Response B: In theory, this is a good activity for launching the day's discussion of the extended reading assignment. However, if students have not been asked to prepare by jotting down questions that occur to them as they read, this activity is may not meet the instructor goals presented in the stem. This activity is also more appropriate for an oral language focus.
- Response C: A daily objective quiz could help the teacher determine whether students are reading their assignments; however, an objective quiz is not the best method of assessing the students' *understanding* of characters' actions and events. Most discussions of assessment discourage the use of objective quizzes to test students' understanding of literary texts.
- Response D: Bringing newspaper clippings to class is a good way to help students find connections between the real world and literature. However, this activity would be more appropriate as a follow-up activity once students have demonstrated they understand the characters and events in the story. This response moves away from the focus of the stem.

Response A best addresses the specifications of the stem.

## 8-12 Practice Item: Literature

(1) A high school English teacher wants to guide students in recognizing how character motivation impacts plot events. (2) Students are reading Edgar Allan Poe's "The Cask of Amontillado" (1846). (3) Which of the following activities would most effectively achieve this goal?

A. Students discuss how their understanding of the characters changes after watching a film version of the story.

B. Students write a character journal in which they take on the role of one of the characters writing journal entries about the events in the story.

✗ C. Students write an essay discussing alternative actions each character could have undertaken and explaining how these actions would have impacted the development of plot events.

✗ D. Students work in groups to present dramatized versions of important events in the plot.

*Analysis.*  This is a literary analysis item focused on the connection between character motivation and plot. Although a particular literary work is mentioned, the responses below indicate that no familiarity with the work is required to pick the correct response.

- Response A: This is a typical, productive activity for teaching literature. However, the stem focuses on understanding character rather than comparing responses to the print and film version of the story. Finally, incorporating a film version of the story is a media literacy rather than a literature activity.
- Response B: Character journals provide a versatile format for students to delve into the character as the plot events occur. While the student's own interpretation of events is required for creation of a character journal, the journal format offers students the opportunity to demonstrate they can connect character motivation and plot events.
- Response C: Writing an essay is a good activity for demonstrating students' understanding of the tightly woven connection between characters' actions and plot events. It also involves critical thinking since the writer must move beyond the literary text to hypothetical scenarios involving the characters. But because it moves beyond the text in the specifications to propose alternative actions, it loses the focus called for in the item stem.
- Response D: Dramatizing events of a story is a good activity for engaging students in the text and for promoting oral language in the class. However, it lacks pointed attention to the focal elements in the item stem, the connection between character motivation and plot events.

Response B best addresses the specifications of the stem.

## Additional Study Strategies for Literature Preparation

### Familiarity with Literature for Your Certification Level

To adequately prepare for your level of TExES, you should know titles and authors of literary texts appropriate for your certification level.

---

**TEST PREP TIP 10: KNOW THE LITERATURE YOUR STUDENTS WILL READ**   As a TExES study strategy, become familiar with the titles, authors, and plots of literary texts typically taught in your certification area. Make sure your research into typically taught books includes traditional and new canonical titles. Because students often draw on previous experiences with literature to shape their response to new literature, you should be familiar with children's and young adult literature that students are likely to have read in earlier grades.

---

At the EC-4 level, this means knowing major titles and authors in children's literature; at the 4-8 level, titles and authors in young adult literature; and at the 8-12 level, traditional canonical works as well as works that have recently been added to the curriculum to reflect diversity and cultural awareness. In the discussion of Test Prep Tip 8: Know the Texts Your Students Will Read in Chapter 2, I suggest several strategies for finding out what texts may be in your curriculum (and by extension, might be mentioned in TExES objective items). Those suggestions apply to literary texts as well, so review that section of Chapter 2 in the context of the information offered in this chapter. For a quick overview of some titles, authors, themes, and plots in children's literature, I suggest Anita Silvey's *100 Best Books for Children* (2004). If you are an 8-12 TExES candidate, do not dismiss this book as irrelevant to your teacher preparation; to be an effective high school teacher of literature, you need to be familiar with the literary texts your students have read in earlier grades.

## 8-12 Literature Content Items

If you are preparing for the ELA/Reading 8-12 TExES, you will be tested on two other aspects of literature beyond pedagogy: (1) your content knowledge of literature (literary periods, literary terminology, and analytical skills), and (2) your writing skills and ability to write analytically about literature. Unfortunately, the literature content objective items are difficult to prepare for if you do not have a firm grounding in literature. Whereas you can figure out or intelligently "guess" at the correct responses to items about teaching literature by analyzing the stem and four responses, in content-knowledge items, you either know the answer or you don't. Still, there are some study strategies you can use to get ready for these types of items.

   First, I recommend that you obtain a copy of Harmon and Holman's *A Handbook to Literature* (2003), now in the ninth edition but even a slightly older edition will be helpful. This book, included in the Selected Resources list at the end of this chapter, should be on every English teacher's resource shelf, so you won't be consulting it only to prepare for the TExES. If you're not familiar with it, the book is basically a "dictionary" of literary terms, most of which have extensive definitions with helpful examples. In addition, it includes a timeline of British and American literature that will enable you to position specific authors or works within a literary or historical period. This timeline is an invaluable study aid for preparing for the 8-12 ELA/Reading TExES. This literature timeline will help you review your understanding of what literary works are associated with particular literary eras, social movements, and historical periods. If we use the practice test included in the ELA/Reading 8-12 TExES Preparation Manual as an indicator of what might be on the actual test, we can assume that there will be questions that ask about features attributed to particular literary periods and movements, about features attributed to particular literary genres, and about the way literary elements contribute to the meaning of a literary passage. The Harmon and Holman book will be a good resource for last-minute test preparation.

A second study strategy is a quick review of the anthologies from your survey courses. Anthologies are generally of two types: the ones that are organized by literary or historical periods, such as the Norton anthologies, and the ones that are organized by literary terms (e.g., diction, style, theme, figures of speech). Kirszner and Mandell's *Literature: Reading, Reacting, Writing* (2004), included in the Selected Resources section at the end of this chapter, is an excellent example of the second type of anthology. You should read a little from these anthologies every night, whether in structured study time or as bedtime reading. You'll be surprised how quickly you'll be able to recall much of the knowledge you acquired in your literature surveys and specialized course if you spend a little time each day with these anthologies.

The third study strategy is to familiarize yourself with the structure of the sample test items for literature content knowledge. Some literature content items test your knowledge of key literary terms, genres, periods, and other concepts by posing direct questions about those terms. Other literature content items require an analysis of a passage with questions about specific aspects of the passage (such as literary devices, features attributed to the genre, attitudes characteristic of the historical period in which the passage was written). Here are some response strategies for literature content items:

- You should not try to respond to items that include a literary passage by reading the item first and then skimming the literary passage for the right answer. Such items require analytical rather than superficial reading of the passage. You need to remember that a literary passage cannot be skimmed as if it were an informative text; you have to pay attention to all the nuances of the language in order to reach a feasible conclusion about the meaning and the artistry of the passage.
- Make sure you focus on the aspect of the passage specified by the stem. Notice that these items require technical knowledge of literature (e.g., literary terms, genre, literary periods) as well as analytical abilities.
- Carefully read through all the responses to ensure that you haven't selected the response hastily and incorrectly.
- Finally, be realistic about your ability to determine which is the correct response. If you do not know the answer even after reading the passage

carefully or after considering the specifications of the stem, do not spend a lot of time trying to figure it out.

*8-12 Literature Exercise.*    The following practice item is representative of the types of literature content items you are likely to encounter on the actual ELA/Reading 8-12 TExES. Note that it is impossible to "figure out" the correct response using the strategies that you will be using for the pedagogy items.

> (1) *Beowulf, The Iliad, The Odyssey,* and *Paradise Lost* are considered literary epics. (2) Which of the following features do these works share that allow us to designate them as epics?
>
> A. Divine intervention in human events, a romantic setting, and a tragic hero whose downfall occurs because of a fatal character flaw.
> B. Events set in the context of a war being fought to save the integrity of a great nation, with each main character contributing both to the resolution and continuation of the war.
> C. A vast setting, an exalted tone and style, and a hero of almost superhuman stature.
> D. A story that retells the origins of a powerful nation, with the founding figures of the nation functioning as the central characters.

*Analysis.*    The two sentences of the item stem clearly delineate this item as a definition item: Your task is to find the correct definition of "epic" among the four responses and to not be misled by the "distractors."

- Response A: You should eliminate this response at least tentatively because of the third characteristic in the list: The "tragic hero" is a feature of *tragedy* rather than the epic.
- Response B: While some epics do in fact take place in a wartime setting, this is not a prerequisite for the epic.
- Response C: This list of characteristics is incomplete if we want a full listing of the features of the epic, but it accurately identifies key features of the genre. This is the only response that identifies features that can be attributed to every literary work that we classify as an epic.
- Response D: The founding of a nation would constitute an event of vast significance, but the additional feature listed in this response (the central characters are the founding fathers of the nation) makes this definition too specific to apply to all epics.

Response C best fits the requirements of the item stem.

## The TExES Essay

The essay you will have to write for the 8-12 TExES calls for a simple, straightforward response strategy. You will compare two passages with a similar theme, so the most pragmatic approach is to handle the essay as a comparison/contrast theme. However, you should not underestimate the difficulty of writing an essay in addition to reading and responding to 90 challenging objective items in a testing period of approximately four hours. Test Prep Tip 11 suggests that you do as much as you can to prepare for the writing task you will face on the 8-12 TExES.

---

**TEST PREP TIP 11: PREPARE FOR THE 8-12 TExES ESSAY**    Make sure you understand the specifications of the TExES essay, familiarize yourself with the scoring rubric, and write a practice essay.

---

As a long-time time teacher of writing and literature, I advise you to be realistic about the demands of the TExES essay. You are likely to feel hampered by the lack of a word processor; by the limit of four booklet pages for writing the essay; by the lack of time to go through planning, drafting, and revising adequately; and by the pressure of writing in a limited time period. To ensure that you do not write the essay hurriedly in the last 30 minutes of the exam period, consider writing a draft or at least a good outline *before* attempting the objective items. Allow yourself approximately 45 minutes at the beginning of the testing period to read the passages, circle or underline "quotable" segments in the passages that you can incorporate into your essay, and write a draft or detailed outline. You won't actually be given scratch paper for a draft, but there is plenty of usable space in the test booklet (the bottom of the pages on which the prompts appear, the backs of other pages, etc.). The draft will also help you fit the complete essay on the four pages allotted in the essay booklet; you will be able to adjust your handwriting to meet the four-page restriction. Writing a draft or outline at the outset of the exam period will allow you to work in an incubation period as you respond to the objective items, and when you return to the draft in the last hour of the testing period, you will be able to see it with fresh eyes and make appropriate revisions.

The ELA/Reading 8-12 Test Preparation Manual includes a rubric that shows you how your essay will be scored on a four-point scale with 4 as the top score; you should study this rubric to ensure that you know what will be expected of you and to avoid incorporating elements in your essay that violate the criteria in the rubric. I have a few other bits of advice to help you do well on your essay and to manage the stress you will undoubtedly feel as you write it.

(1) Put a title on the essay.
(2) Keep the essay structure simple. Begin with a very short introductory paragraph that names the two authors and the titles of the passages and that specifies the theme you will discuss. The body should be a straightforward comparison/contrast structure, one or two paragraphs per passage. Make sure you give equal attention to both passages. In other words, do not write 350 words on one passage and only 75 on the other. And end with a conclusion, even if it's only a sentence or two in length.

(3) Refer to the authors as you discuss the passage. Make sure you get the gender right if you're using pronouns. If you can't tell from the name whether the author is male or female, write your sentences so that you do not have to use a pronoun to refer to the author. Use only the author's last name following the initial mention of the whole name; do not use "Mr." or any feminine form of address in referring to the authors.

(4) Use carefully selected, short quotations from the passages to support your observations. Remember you only have four pages in which to present your essay, so do not use up your valuable space on long quotations from the passage. The graders of your essay are likely to dismiss long quotations as evidence that you are unable to write effectively about the passages.

(5) Use appropriate literary terms to discuss the passage (e.g., imagery, metaphor, diction, symbolism, point of view). Make sure you use the terms correctly and distinctly, but do not define the terms. Instead, use your discussion to illustrate your understanding of these terms in the context of the passages.

(6) Try to focus on a single, salient literary element in your discussion of the passages. If you try to mention every literary element you detect, your essay will seem fragmented and incoherent.

(7) The prompt requirements call for an analytical essay, which means that first person commentary about your reactions to the work is inappropriate. If you want to discuss reaction to the passages elicited by the authors' choices in literary devices, refer to "the reader" or use the general first person, "we."

(8) Pace yourself so that you don't end up leaving out part of your essay because you run out of time.

(9) Leave yourself a few minutes to proofread your essay.

The sample essay in Figure 4.2 is written in response to the prompt in the test booklet. Notice the marginal comments that explain how each part of the essay works to fulfill the requirements of the prompt. Think of the sample as a model of what your essay should look like and use it to direct your own writing effort.

## Attempting the Practice Items

If you have not already worked through the literature sample items in your TExES Preparation Manual, you should attempt them now. Identify them by looking at the test competency printed at the bottom of each page. Since there are no separate test competencies for literature at the EC-4 or 4-8 levels, identify the literature sample items by matching the content of the item to the terms and concepts discussed in this chapter. For example, an EC-4 item that deals with theme or character in a story should be considered a literature item.

## FIGURE 4.2   Sample TExES Essay

| Text | Comments |
|---|---|
| **Society's Workers: Exploitation or Societal Necessity?**<br><br>In the passage from Charles Dickens' novel *Hard Times* and in Martin Espada's poem "Who Burns for the Perfection of Paper," irony is used to convey the theme that menial labor, while vital to maintain a society, goes unacknowledged and unappreciated by those who reap the benefits of those efforts. | *The title reflects the student writer's focus in the essay. The authors' names, the titles of the works, and the genres are written into the opening sentence. The writer specifies a literary device: irony. The theme is stated.* |
| Espada's poem moves from a description of work in a paper factory to the unexpected image of the narrator as law school student. The result of this juxtaposition is irony: The law student who is using legal pads to take class notes knows the physical pain that had to be endured to produce them. The narrator knows about the paper cuts "thinner than the crevices/of the skin" that sting from the glue "till both palms burned." The narrator is a "privileged" user of the law pads—it is unlikely that the typical law student would contemplate the genesis of the yellow pads on which are written the notes that will eventually support the law degree. The narrator's experience is ironic: There is no indication that, when the narrator worked in the paper factory, he/she had aspirations to attend law school. Thus, when we, the readers, learn in the second stanza that "Ten years later, in law school" the narrator has special knowledge of the labor and pain production of the legal pads required, we see the irony: The effort in the paper factory—a mere laborer's effort—supports the effort of the law student—a member of the elite in the society. | *This paragraph discusses Espada's poem only.*<br><br>*The writer explains how the images in the poem create irony.*<br><br>*Several well-chosen quotations are used to support the points.* |
| Dickens' commentary on the apparent indifference of the "haves" to the sacrifices of the "have nots" points to the exploitation of workers—the lowest rung of society—for the benefit of the elite. Dickens' workers function in a work-a-day-world of black canals, rivers polluted by ill-smelling dyes, and buildings that tremble all day because of the machinery that keeps industry going. Dickens points to the monotony of the lives and days of the workers: "streets very like one another," "streets more like one another," "inhabited by people equally like one another." And the repetitive, unending motion of the piston that keeps everything going he says is "like the head of an elephant in a state of melancholy madness." Coketown is like a colony of ants, creatures characterized by their industry, by their blind commitment to their appointed tasks, by their ceaseless labor, and by their uniformity. Coketown, writes Dickens, "was inhabited by people equally like one another . . . [who] do the same work" and for whom every day is just like the next. These images result in irony when Dickens shows us a "fine lady" who can "scarcely bear to hear [Coketown] mentioned" and who is oblivious to the labor and sacrifice it takes to sustain her lifestyle and her comfort. | *This paragraph discusses the Dickens passage only.*<br><br>*Here, also, the focus is on how the images create irony.*<br><br>*Quotations from the passage are used to support the writer's points.* |
| Dickens' and Espada's ironic tone, created by images that juxtapose the worker and the oblivious beneficiary of the labor, causes discomfort in the reader. They create images of workers functioning like automatons—not aware of who will reap the fruits of their labor but knowing full well that they themselves will not benefit from their work. Espada's poem leaves us with the image of hands bloodied and burning from paper cuts sustained in producing legal pads that will help prospective attorneys on their way to fortune, prestige, and status. The dispassionate voice in which Coketown is described underscores the monotony, the repetitiveness, the hopelessness of life for the worker. It must continue this way ("fact, fact, fact, everywhere in the material aspect of the town"); otherwise, society will crumble. The passage ends, ironically, with a prayer-like closing: "World without end, Amen." Nothing can be done to "right" the situation if society is to thrive: The exploited worker is a vital part of an ordered society. Without the bloody hands that produce the legal pads, without the workers in the polluted factories, society cannot survive. It is the way it must be if society is to survive. | *The closing paragraph brings together the two passages, linking the common theme to the irony seen in both passages. The essay is tightly controlled, with the closing echoing the ideas introduced in the first paragraph.*<br><br>*This paragraph both continues the discussion of the theme and concludes the essay—a good strategy if you are able to work it out this way.* |

REFLECTION FOR YOUR TExES JOURNAL:   Having worked through the information and exercises in this chapter, how prepared do you feel for the literature portion of your TExES exam? Do you feel particularly insecure about any of the types of information you are expected to know in literature content and pedagogy? If you are an 8-12 candidate, how confident do you feel about your ability to write a level 4 essay? What specific goals have you set to continue your preparation for this segment of the exam?

# Chapter Summary

- Each TExES level requires a different type of preparation for the literature component. Make sure that you follow the strategies suggested in this chapter to be optimally prepared for the literature section of the actual TExES exam you will be taking.
- Familiarize yourself with the literary texts the students at your certification level are likely to be reading for class assignments.
- If you feel deficient in particular literature categories discussed in this chapter, read some of the Selected Resources.
- If you are taking the ELA/Reading 8-12 TExES, write at least one practice essay prior to taking the actual test, using the sample essay in Figure 4.2 as a model.

# Selected Resources: Literature Content and Pedagogy

Most of the suggested readings included here have been selected because of the way they illustrate pedagogical principles and practices that will prepare you to understand the teaching scenarios that may show up in TExES objective items. The articles integrate terminology found in TEKS and educator standards. Although each article is written in response to situations at particular grade levels, for the most part, the activities are adaptable to all teaching levels. Finally, if you have had no literature methods courses or courses in which you spent some class time discussing approaches to teaching literature, you should read the literature chapters in at least one of the books included in the Comprehensive Resources section of Chapter 1.

Burke, C. L., & Copenhaver, J. G. (2004). Animals as people in children's literature. *Language Arts 81*(3), 205-213.
> Burke's and Copenhaver's discussion of the use of animals (or inanimate objects) as characters in children's literature is set in the context of anthropomorphism as a means of dealing with difficult social and personal issues. The authors provide synopses of many literary texts in which animals appear as characters.

Bushman, J. H. (1997). Young adult literature in the classroom—Or is it? *English Journal 86*(3), 35-40.

> Bushman begins by pointing out that many if not most of the traditional literary works typically taught in middle and senior high school English classes do not meet the students' personal and psychological needs and consequently fail to engage the readers and foster an interest in literature. Bushman's underlying premise—that literature should help adolescent students forge their personal identities—reflects TEKS and educator standard statements about the importance of helping students find connections between literature and their lives. Of pragmatic value for the TExES candidate are Bushman's summaries of traditional and young adult texts taught in middle and senior high school.

Cope, J. (1998). Why I teach, promote, and love adolescent literature: Confessions of a college English professor. *Voices from the Middle 5*(2), 7-9.

> Cope offers strong arguments for the value of young adult literature, pointing out that YA literature can serve as a bridge for moving students toward appreciation of the "classics." Using examples from several YA books, Cope shows how the characters and the treatment of themes engage adolescents in a way that traditional literature does not. Cope's language reflects terms and concepts found in the reading/literary response sections of TEKS.

Greenbaum, V. (1997). Beyond the bookroom: Modern literature, modern literacy, and the teaching of Annie Proulx' *The Shipping News. English Journal 86*(8), 17-20.

> Greenbaum's article begins with a brief but highly informative discussion of the literary canon that she uses to support her inclusion of contemporary author Annie Proulx's *The Shipping News* in her high school class curriculum. Familiarity with the novel is not necessary for understanding Greenbaum's article; she offers well-chosen excerpts from the novel to explain the activities she describes. The activities are designed to help students connect with the literary text, to make the language accessible, and to respond to the text—all of which reflect the language of TEKS and educator standards.

Harmon, W., & Holman H. (2003). *A handbook to literature* (9th ed.). Upper Saddle River, NJ: Prentice Hall.

> This is helpful for brushing up your knowledge of major literary terms and concepts. Refer to the Reading/culture, Reading/literary response, and Reading/literary concepts TEKS for terms and concepts that you might reference in this handbook. If you are preparing for the 8-12 TExES, make sure you read the entries for "Periods of English and American Literary History" as well as the "Outline of Literary History: British and American" at the back of the book.

Kirszner, L. G., & Mandell, S. R. (2004). *Literature: Reading, reacting, writing* (5th ed.). Boston: Heinle.

> This is a literature content resource. You would use this book to refresh your knowledge of literature titles, story plots, literary elements, and literary devices. Kirszner and Mandell offer a good mix of traditional, contemporary, and new-to-the-canon selections, so the 8-12 TExES candidate will find this resource useful in understanding TEKS and educator standards on general knowledge of literature, literary analysis, and literature and culture. Includes a short but helpful glossary of literary terms.

Maloch, B. (2004). One teacher's journey: Transitioning into literature discussion groups. *Language Arts 81*(4), 312-322.

> This article provides an extended discussion of how literature circles are implemented in a third-grade classroom; however, the rationale and strategies offered by Maloch are applicable to any level of ELA teaching. Maloch shows how teachers can guide students to become independent readers of literary texts as a result of participating in literature discussion groups. Much of what is covered in the article is a demonstration of how oral language skills can be integrated into the teaching of literature in order to develop skills that heighten students' appreciation of literature: posing questions about literary texts, devel-

oping critical response abilities, negotiating with other readers about interpretations of a text, maintaining a high level of engagement with a text, and critically evaluating one's own response to a text—all of which reflect TEKS and educator standards expectations.

Matthews, R., & Chandler, R. (1998). Using reader response to teach *Beloved* in a high school American studies classroom. *English Journal 88*(2), 85-92.

Matthews and Chandler begin the article with a cogent argument for increasing diversity in our literature selections by incorporating culturally rich texts such as Toni Morrison's *Beloved*. They consider this a "challenging" text, so many of the activities they describe are aimed at making the text accessible to students. Major sections of the article describe activities that reflect pedagogical practices and principles for teaching literature effectively: pre-reading, reading, and postreading. The authors include examples of student responses to each activity described.

Probst, R. (2000). Literature as invitation. *Voices from the Middle 8*(2), 8-15.

Probst describes several strategies that encourage students to talk about literature. The activities highlight dialogue—where students begin by expressing their own responses to literary texts and then move toward listening to others' responses and eventually constructing meaning based on the intellectual inquiry that results from dialogue. A particularly interesting and versatile activity is the "passing notes" adaptation. Probst suggests teachers take advantage of students' interest in passing notes to each other during class and adapt this urge to passing notes about literature. This article should help TExES candidates at all certification levels understand what is meant by the reading/literary response TEKS.

Silvey, A. (2004). *100 best books for children*. Boston: Houghton Mifflin.

This book is a great resource for TExES candidates who have had no course work in children's or young adult literature. While it is not a theoretical book, it does offer significant insights into the themes, characters, and situations in children's books. Silvey provides background information about the author, the circumstances of publication, and other interesting tidbits on each book in addition to a brief summary of the plot. The books are categorized according to the reader's age, starting with board books for prereaders to books for older readers.

Sklar, S. M. (2002). Shall we bury Caesar or praise him? Ideas for the revitalization of an old standard. *English Journal 92*(1), 36-40.

This article begins with the author's candid acknowledgment that many secondary English teachers dread teaching Shakespeare's *Julius Caesar* because of difficulties in helping students relate to the play and understand the language. Sklar describes numerous creative and pedagogically sound teaching activities for engaging students as they read *Caesar*. Possibly the most compelling activity presented in this article is the connection of Caesar's assassination in the play to the assassinations of major political figures in the United States through student interviews with adults who remember those assassinations. Sklar's activities clearly reflect the knowledge that test takers are expected to have about helping students find connections to literature, about integrating film into the teaching of literature, and about providing opportunities for students to do oral interpretations of literary works.

Thomas, P. L. (1998). "It beckons, and it baffles—": Resurrecting Emily Dickinson (and poetry) in the student-centered classroom. *English Journal 87*(3), 60-63.

A key activity in Thomas's approach to teaching Emily Dickinson is showing how REM's song lyrics can be used as a bridge to comprehending poetry that may seem irrelevant to students' lives. The Dickinson unit ends with students writing their own poems in the tone and style of Dickinson; the article includes several student poems.

Van Horn, L. (2000). Young adult literature: An entry into the joys of reading. *Voices in the Middle 8*(2). 40-47.

Van Horn explains and illustrates how young adult literature helps adolescents appreciate literary language and structures and learn about their own emotions—goals that reflect TEKS Reading/literary response and Reading/literary concepts sections. Van Horn describes numerous class activities that she uses to encourage young readers to engage personally and critically with the YA novels they are reading such as staging chapters of the book, creating a similar story in a different setting, drawing life-size images of characters in YA novels, finding real-life "characters" that reflect the features of characters in the YA novel, writing poems in the voice of characters from the novel, and creating scrapbooks that might have been put together by a character. Much of Van Horn's article focuses on activities she uses in teaching S. E. Hinton's *The Outsiders,* so TExES candidates will have an extended view of what is involved in teaching a YA novel.

# 5 Oral Language

Once upon a time, oral language was considered the exclusive domain of speech teachers, with language arts restricted more or less to writing, grammar, reading, and literature instruction. As researchers and theorists have observed and reported that English language arts are integrated processes, ELA has expanded to include, as Nancy Rost Goulden (1998) explains, "not only the traditional language arts of writing and reading but also the 'new' language arts of speaking, listening, and media literacy" (p. 90). TEKS and educator standards clearly reflect this attitude. At every grade level, there are several TEKS categories devoted to listening/speaking, and each certification level has educator standards in oral language and oral communication. The integration of oral language into the ELA curriculum has caused us to examine what it is that makes classroom talk effective and productive. Although we will be looking at specific components of oral language in this chapter, in actuality, oral language is integrated into every aspect of ELA classroom interactions since almost every moment of our classroom activities is launched by oral language, beginning with the teacher's greeting to her students. Thus, in actual classroom practice, it would be quite difficult to isolate oral language from other language arts.

## Oral Language: An Overview

Let's begin our preparation for the oral language component of TExES by considering a working definition of the term.

ORAL LANGUAGE: A WORKING DEFINITION   Oral language encompasses listening and speaking processes used in classrooms to promote learning. Despite the pervasiveness of speaking and listening interactions in the classroom, effective use of oral language requires knowledge of principles and strategies that enables us to use this important language art to enhance students' learning in all language arts and in all other disciplines.

Listening and speaking are considered *processes,* which suggests that there are repeatable, teachable steps to these two language arts components. Thinking of listening and speaking as processes also requires that we view these language arts critically—we need to identify those practices that help us communicate more effectively via oral language and devise classroom activities and approaches that promote listening and speaking competence.

In the context of TEKS and educator standards, the listening and speaking processes are means of helping students become productive members of classroom communities and other social and academic groups in which oral communication skills are required. Oral language skills include the following:

- Questioning skills
- Spontaneous talk in the classroom
- Giving directions
- Small group interactions
- Whole group discussions
- Debating skills
- Mock trials
- Interviewing
- Critical listening
- Critiques of oral presentations
- Formal speeches

This list is not exhaustive; it is intended to give you an idea of what you need to know about the oral language component of English language arts instruction. Keep in mind, as well, that oral language is considered a discipline on its own. In colleges and universities, oral language is the domain of communication departments; in public schools, oral language is managed in speech and drama classes. In the context of TExES preparation, however, we will be looking only at the way we integrate selected oral language components into the universe of language arts instruction.

---

**REFLECTION FOR YOUR TEXES JOURNAL:**   Think about your "classroom talk." Do you like asking questions and offering comments in class? What guidelines do you use for shaping your oral responses and questions in class? How often do you address classmates instead of the teacher? Do you get nervous when you have to make an oral presentation? What strategies do you use to reduce your anxiety when you have to speak in front of a group?

---

## Coordinating Oral Language Study Materials

To organize the listening and speaking categories from TEKS, educator standards, and test competencies, let's designate orange as the color code for oral language. Mark and flag the following oral language sections:

- TEKS: all listening/speaking category headings
- Educator standards and test competencies that address oral language or oral communication
- Sample test items: All items related to oral language and oral communication test competencies (look for the test competencies at the bottom of each sample test item in the preparation manual).

Figure 5.1 shows you how to correlate these components and how to determine what courses might be relevant to your oral language preparation.

At this point, you should read through the correlated components to familiarize yourself with the terms and concepts associated with teaching listening and speaking in the context of the ELA classroom.

**FIGURE 5.1    Oral Language Study Chart**

| EC-4 | | | |
| --- | --- | --- | --- |
| **TEKS K-4** | **Educator Standards** | **Test Competencies** | **Relevant Courses** |
| Listening/speaking/purposes<br>Listening/speaking/culture<br>Listening/speaking/audience/<br>  oral grammar<br>Listening/speaking/communication<br>Listening/speaking/critical listening | Standard I. Oral Language | Competency 001<br>(Oral Language) | Emergent literacy<br>Literacy development<br>Speech/Communication |

| 4-8 | | | |
| --- | --- | --- | --- |
| **TEKS Grades 4 & 5**<br>**TEKS Middle School** | **Educator Standards** | **Test Competencies** | **Relevant Courses** |
| Listening/speaking/purposes<br>Listening/speaking/critical listening<br>Listening/speaking/appreciation<br>Listening/speaking/culture<br>Listening/speaking/audiences | Standard I. Oral Language | Competency 001<br>(Oral Language) | Literacy development<br>Speech/Communication |

| 8-12 | | | |
| --- | --- | --- | --- |
| **TEKS Grade 8**<br>**TEKS High School** | **Educator Standards** | **Test Competencies** | **Courses** |
| Listening/speaking/critical listening<br>Listening/speaking/evaluation<br>Listening/speaking/purposes<br>Listening/speaking/presentations<br>Listening/speaking/literary<br>  interpretations | Standard VIII | Competency 010 | Literacy development<br>Speech/Communication |

REFLECTION FOR YOUR TEXES JOURNAL: As you read through TEKS, educator standards, and sample test items in oral language, jot down key terms and terms you do not know. As you continue working through this chapter, make sure you find definitions and explanations for the terms you do not understand.

# A Glossary of Selected Oral Language Terms and Concepts

If you have taken speech or communication courses in college, you should take out the books you used for those courses and look up glossary terms for which you want further explanation.

**active listening:**   A learned skill. Teachers need to provide guidance for students to become active listeners just as they need to provide guidance for active reading. Active listening requires that students adopt strategies such as taking notes, asking questions during discussions if appropriate, addressing comments and questions to classmates during class discussions, and using body language and facial expressions that indicate they are listening.

**authentic communication:**   A classroom interaction that students find meaningful and/or relevant. Oral communication is authentic when students are encouraged to participate as members of the discourse community that has been formed in the classroom. In authentic communication, students feel their voices and ideas matter; students learn how to respond productively to ideas with which they disagree; they learn to negotiate; they learn to value others' ideas.

**classroom talk:**   The oral language interactions that occur in classrooms. "[W]hat we do in class is largely talk," writes Leila Christenbury (2000, p. 248). We engage in small talk with students; we give directions; we correct inappropriate or disruptive behavior; we respond to questions; we lecture; we make jokes, we have student-teacher conferences; we comment on campus events; we participate in class discussions; and we offer all sorts of directions. When we make oral language a language art, we take on the responsibility of helping our students learn to talk and to listen productively in classroom settings and, by extension, in other social settings. The classroom, then, becomes a training ground for students to discover and refine the arts of speaking and listening effectively.

**composing process (for formal speeches):**   A composing process virtually identical to the writing process. There must be a prewriting stage that could include research. The drafting and revising stages will include preparation of the actual text as well as incorporation of elements designed to affect the audience. In oral communication, however, the publication stage is the delivery of the speech, and this stage must incorporate the student's knowledge of how voice projection, intonation, body language, visual props, and technology can be used to enhance the presentation of the speech.

**conventions of oral language:**   Practices and listener expectations that should be integrated into speeches and extemporaneous oral language productions. You might best understand what this term means by thinking about the conventions of *written* language. When you write, there are things you do automatically to ensure your reader doesn't get confused; for example, you indent or double space to indicate a paragraph break, you paginate your pages, you capitalize the first word of each sentence, and so on. In oral language, conventions are practices such as avoiding excessively long or complex sentences because they are difficult for a listener to process, avoiding a monotone, using appropriate voice modulations, speaking clearly and distinctly, speaking at a pace the listener can follow, using organizational signals (like *first, another, as we draw to a close*), maintaining eye contact with members of the audience, and not fidgeting with hair, jewelry, or clothing during delivery of a presentation.

**critical listening:**   The ability to evaluate a spoken message by, among other things, determining the speaker's purpose, identifying the speaker's message, analyzing rhetorical strategies, recognizing persuasive appeals, distinguishing between fact and opinion, posing questions, and accurately identifying main points in the speaker's message. Simply put, critical listening means active listening, listening to gain information and/or to participate in the "conversation" that might result from an oral language interaction. Students need to be taught to listen critically. Students need to know how to apply critical listening skills outside the classroom as they have conversations with friends, interact with parents and other adults, listen to television newscasts, attend social events where formal and informal speeches are included, and listen to televised political speeches.

**critiques:**   A device for helping students become active listeners during group or individual oral presentations. Critique sheets specify the criteria on which the speech and speaker will be evaluated. Critique sheets can be developed by the teacher or collaboratively with students. Knowing ahead of time on what basis they will be evaluated enables presenters to adjust their speeches or presentations to meet the specifications of the critique sheet.

**culture:**   Behaviors that reflect students' familial and cultural expectations. Teachers should be aware that students' cultural backgrounds significantly affect their oral language interactions in the classroom. Habitual silence from a student, for example, should not automatically be perceived as lack of preparedness or disinterest; in some cultures, quiet participation shows respect for the speaker/authority. Teachers should strive to create classroom environments in which cultural norms about participation in communities (such as a classroom community) are respected.

**debate:**   A highly structured oral language activity in which students take sides on an important issue, devise propositions, and then use specific types of evidence to support the propositions. A debate is a formal, argumentative event that requires considerable expertise on the part of the coach or teacher to ensure that students observe the "rules" of debating. If you have limited training in debating, you can still use debates in your ELA classroom as a means of developing your students' oral language skills. An informal debate can be an opportunity for students to examine character motivation in a literary work or, in a current events setting, to analyze opposing viewpoints in important political or social issues. A formal debate would rise above the specific events in the novel and look specifically at the issues raised by the events (e.g., freedom of speech, constitutional rights).

**dramatizing:**   A type of oral language activity. Dramatizing also involves *role playing*. There are many different ways to use dramatizing in the ELA classroom. For example, students can act out scenes from plays; they can subdivide novels or short stories into "scene-like" segments and act them out; they can read a poem dramatically, incorporating gestures, movements, and appropriate intonation and volume to convey the meaning. Dramatizing fosters creativity and socializing skills.

**extemporaneous speech:**   A type of oral presentation in which preparation is minimal and students must organize ideas and content quickly and present the speech without referring to notes. This is comparable to writing on demand where students must use different strategies for preparation and submission of an essay from those they would use in a writing project where more time is available for planning, reflection, and revision. In an ELA classroom, extemporaneous speaking could be used to develop students' audience awareness skills and organization skills.

**fishbowl:**   A type of class discussion in which students are arranged into two concentric circles, with the outer circle serving as observers of students in the inner circle during a discussion. Fishbowl discussions can be used to develop oral language skills. Typically, in a fishbowl discussion, only the students in the inner circle participate in the discussion while the students in the outer circle listen to the discussion and critically note the dynamics of the inner circle's interactions. After the discussion is over, the outer circle talks about their observations and analyzes the inner circle participants' contributions to the discussion.

**formal presentation:**   An oral presentation in which students are evaluated on the quality of the performance as well as the quality of the content. These presentations usually are prepared over an extended period of time and may require significant research and preparation; presentations may be done by groups or individuals. Students have specific, detailed instructions from the teacher in formal oral presentations.

**gender:**   A significant concern in oral language classroom activities. Research shows that male students elicit higher levels of attention from teachers than do female students. Keep in mind that this generalization is based on controlled classroom research; what you yourself have observed may not seem consistent with this conclusion. The point is that there are documented differences between the way male and female students utilize their oral language skills in the classroom. Maxwell and Meiser suggest that "we be more conscious of how we acknowledge and respond to our male and female students, or risk continuing patterns of gender inequity that research has recently uncovered" (2005, p. 122).

**groups:**   One of the most common ways of incorporating oral language into the ELA classroom. For group work to be productive, teachers should follow a few guidelines. (1) The number of students in each group should be carefully regulated. There is no "magic" optimum number of group members, but a "group" of fewer than three members is not really a group; five is usually considered an upper limit because more members than that makes the group unwieldy. (2) The teacher needs to clearly delineate the group's assignment. Groups should not be given a general assignment, such as, "Discuss Poe's 'The Cask of Amontillado.'" Instead, the assignment should be specific: "Find clues in the first few paragraphs of 'The Cask of Amontillado' that help us understand the characteristics of Montressor and Fortunato." (3) It is frequently a good idea to have group members decide on a division of labor: One group member can take notes on the group's discussion, another can be in charge of reworking the notes for the presentation, another can be the presenter. (4) Work time should be regulated carefully to meet the specifications of the task. In other words, the teacher should set a time limit on the group interaction and then ask for a status report from each group as the work period draws to a close.

**informal presentations:**   A category of oral presentations. Oral presentations can be very broadly divided into informal or formal presentations. Informal presentations are not as rigorously structured as formal presentations. Usually, informal presentations are embedded as elements of a larger class activity, such as reading a novel or working on a grammar unit, with the informal presentation contributing to the students' understanding of that larger activity.

**interviewing:**   An oral language activity that incorporates questioning skills, audience awareness, problem solving, and role playing. Students should be taught interviewing basics, such as (1) do not ask an interview subject yes or no questions; (2) do not prompt the interviewee by asking leading questions (such as, "Don't you agree that our football team could have performed better this season?"); (3) make sure you listen to the interviewee's responses so that you can ask follow-up questions if appropriate; (4) have a set of questions prepared ahead of time but do not rigidly stick to the scripted questions if an opportunity presents itself for following an interesting interview strand. Interviews can be used for role-playing in classroom situations or for gathering field data for reports and research.

**nonverbal communication:**   Body language, eye contact, gestures, intonation, inflection, posture, and movement used during an oral language activity or performance. Students should be taught that nonverbal cues can be used to amplify or emphasize aspects of an oral presentation or performance. Similarly, they should be taught that inadvertent use of some types of nonverbal cues (such as fidgeting with hair or jewelry, rocking back and forth, staring at the ceiling, or keeping one's hands in one's pockets) might distract the listener and diminish the impact of the message. In addition, teachers should be sensitive to the way that culture may influence a student's use or understanding of traditional nonverbal cues. Students should also be taught that nonverbal communication is important even in ordinary classroom interactions, such as during teacher-guided lessons; for example, they should be taught that certain nonverbal cues suggest inattentiveness.

**oral interpretation:** Usually, a dramatic reading of a literary or nonfiction text. "Oral" interpretation suggests that only verbal components figure into the interpretation. However, students should be taught that posture, pauses, facial expression, and gestures significantly influence the interpretation. Oral interpretations allow students to use dramatic components to convey the meaning they have constructed, so it is a creative as well as interpretative oral language activity.

**oral presentations:** A type of oral language classroom activity. Oral presentations can be informal (as when a small group discussions culminate in short reports to the class) or formal (as when students work individually or collaboratively to present a structured, well-planned presentation). Teachers should provide guidelines to ensure that students understand the requirements of either type of presentation and to help students use verbal and nonverbal communication effectively.

**public speaking:** Class activities that enable students to manage real public speaking tasks with confidence and competence. Teachers should provide opportunities for students to practice addressing friendly as well as hostile audiences, for creating texts that could be read in various public settings, and for using rhetorical strategies to enhance the impact of a speech. Teachers can utilize role-playing or mock event activities to help students develop public speaking skills, or they can set up real-world public speaking situations.

**purpose for listening:** The rationale or motivation for listening to a particular oral language text. Because listening is a component of communication, we apply the same elements of communication to listening as we do to writing or reading. Thus, we can analyze the listening process on the basis of the message, the audience, and the purpose. We listen for many reasons, but we can broadly categorize those reasons as to gain information, to be entertained, to be persuaded, to appreciate a creative performance, to gain insights on a situation, to hear another point of view.

**questioning skills:** An important aspect of oral communication skills. We need to teach students how to ask productive questions by (1) creating a classroom environment that encourages students to ask questions; (2) respecting students' questions (in other words, by not making students feel foolish for asking questions); (3) helping students learn to ask productive questions; (4) turning student questions into opportunities for teaching; (5) using student questions to foster interactions among students; (6) refraining from making negative comments in response to student questions.

**radio:** A valuable resource for helping students develop listening and speaking skills. Writing scripts for radio and producing mock radio broadcasts can teach students much about audience analysis and about the impact of media. Students should listen to popular radio shows to get a sense of the way that communicating over the radio impacts the development and production of the message. Web sites for popular radio shows, such as Garrison Keillor's *Prairie Home Companion* (included in the Selected Resources at the end of this chapter), offer scripts of the various segments of the show. Reading the script while listening to the segment gives students insights into how the text of the script is "translated" into the actual oral performance that we hear on the radio.

**reader's theater:** An activity designed to promote students' competence and self-confidence during oral reading performances. Students "perform" before an audience of their classmates. They may read from a book or from a script they have prepared; in either case, readers are encouraged to demonstrate engagement with the text by reading dramatically.

**role-playing:** An activity in which students assume roles of fictional characters, historical figures, contemporary celebrities, politicians, or other real or fictitious figures. Role-playing lends authenticity to a learning situation and integrates creativity (as in creative dramatics) into traditional language arts activities. When students pretend to be other people or characters, they must adopt the personality, language style, motivations, and other traits of the person whose role they are assuming.

**scripted speech:**    An oral language activity in which the presenter reads from a prepared text. Students need guidance in learning the difference between a text that is presented orally and one that is intended to be read silently. Teachers should advise students to use strategies intended to keep the listener from getting lost, such as using organizational markers to identify key ideas, avoiding excessively complex syntactic structures, incorporating definitions of key terms, repeating key terms, and selecting details carefully. A scripted speech should be *composed* using writing process stages used for writing essays; the difference is that the final product must be prepared for an audience that will *listen* rather than read.

**student talk/teacher talk:**    A ratio that measures the difference between classroom time devoted to students talking and time taken up by the teacher's talk. Quite a bit of research has been conducted on the ratio between teacher talk and student talk. It would seem appropriate that the teacher should have a higher talk ratio than students, but current theories about classroom interactions suggest that silent students are passive learners. If we think of a classroom as a community of learners, teachers should be talking *with* students as well as talking *to* students. Thus, teachers should devise ways of promoting student talk that leads to questioning, socialization among learners, productive classroom interactions, and learning.

**whole class discussion:**    A discussion led by the teacher, involving questions and answers and comments during or in response to the teacher's lecture or presentation. The descriptor "whole class" is intended to differentiate this type of discussion, in which all class members are participating as a large group, from small group discussions in which the class is divided into smaller groups. Whole class discussions can serve as opportunities for teachers to help students develop questioning skills and to learn to interact with other students in productive ways.

# Classroom Practices: Oral Language

Although speaking and listening are fundamental aspects of all classrooms, there are practices and strategies we can adopt to use classroom talk as an opportunity to develop students' oral language skills.

- The ELA teacher should strive to create a classroom community in which students feel comfortable responding to questions during class discussion and asking questions about material the class is studying or about events and situations external to the classroom.
- When directing a class discussion, the ELA teacher should ask questions that lead to critical thinking.
- The ELA teacher should ensure that students are not embarrassed when they answer questions in a way that the teacher did not anticipate. In other words, teachers should learn to "redirect" student responses that aren't exactly on target toward a response that promotes student understanding of the topic being discussed.
- "Noise" should be a part of every ELA classroom. If we value oral language, we should recognize that talking, laughing, arguing, scraping desks and chairs across the room, whispering, and other actions that might be considered "disruptive" are integral to oral language development. If silence is the opposite of noise, we should strive to create "noisy" classrooms.

REFLECTION FOR YOUR TEXES JOURNAL:   Try to analyze the types of talk that you have experienced in your classrooms, at elementary, secondary, and college levels. Do any instances of particularly effective or particularly disastrous listening-speaking situations stand out in your memory? Identify activities that teachers and/or professors have used that directly or indirectly promoted your oral language competence.

## Test Item Exercises

Let's look at three oral language practice items and an analysis of the strategies for selecting the correct response.

### EC-4 Practice Item: Oral Language

(1) Ms. Luera, a first-grade teacher, wants to develop her students' oral communication skills. (2) She sets up the following scenario for her first graders:

Let's pretend we have new student named Lorrie in our class. I've made picture cards for five different places in the school that Lorrie needs to know how to find: the school library, the nurse's office, the principal's office, the lunch room, and the girls' bathroom. I am going to put you in groups, and each group will have a picture card of the place in our school that your group needs to help Lorrie find. One person from another group will pretend to be Lorrie and she can listen and ask questions as your group members tell her how to get to the school place on your picture card.

(3) This activity best promotes which of the following language arts teaching objectives?

A. To guide students in helping a new student become a member of the classroom community.
B. To help students develop creativity by performing a role-playing task.
C. To provide an opportunity for students to practice oral communication skills in an authentic situation.
D. To encourage shy students to speak clearly and distinctly before an audience.

*Analysis.*   The stem sets up the class activity as one designed to develop quite specific oral communication skills: giving directions. TEKS includes giving directions as an activity that promotes audience awareness and appropriate application of conventions of oral language.

- Response A: Although the teacher's scenario includes a hypothetical new student, the focus of the activity is not socialization but giving directions.
- Response B: The direction-giving activity clearly involves role-playing. If this were an actual test item, you might be tempted to select this one as the right response. However, you need to continue reading all the responses and evaluating the extent to which each meets the specifications of the stem.
- Response C: Practicing oral communication skills might seem to be a simplistic response (and thus you might be tempted to discard it). However, the term "authentic" is a key word in this response: Giving and listening to directions is an important real-world skill. The teacher's scenario allows students to think about how they might respond in a similar situation in real life.
- Response D: The teacher's scenario or activity set up makes no attempt to focus on shy students.

Response C best matches the specifications established by the item stem.

## 4-8 Practice Item: Oral Language

(1) Mr. Allen's seventh-grade class is reading Avi's *Nothing But the Truth* (1991), a young adult novel in which both the 14-year-old-male protagonist, Philip, and his English teacher, Miss Narwin, relocate to different schools by the end of the novel. (2) When Philip hums the National Anthem during morning announcements in Miss Narwin's class, she sends him to the principal, which triggers the chain of events that lead to Miss Narwin's dismissal and Philip's suspension from school. (3) As the novel progresses, the incident escalates into a national discussion about patriotism, classroom discipline, teachers' rights, and students' rights. (4) Mr. Allen gives the class the following assignment.

Imagine you are a member of the community in which *Nothing But the Truth* is set. The local school board is meeting to determine whether Philip or Miss Narwin is in the right. You will work in groups to prepare a speech in defense of the character whose name your group draws. Two groups will prepare speeches in defense of Philip and two other groups in defense of Miss Narwin. You will select one of your group members to deliver the speech before the "school board," which will be made up of eight classmates whose names are randomly drawn from a box containing all your names. At the conclusion of the speeches, the "school board members" will vote on whether to reinstate Philip or Miss Narwin.

(5) This activity would best promote which of the following oral language skills?

A. Students will demonstrate their knowledge of the U.S. Constitution by citing segments of the Bill of Rights as evidence.

    B. Students will demonstrate their ability to analyze audience and select details and evidence designed to influence that audience.

    C. Students will demonstrate their ability to prepare a formal debate on issues that are important in real-world situations.

    D. Students will demonstrate their ability to write a scripted speech.

*Analysis.*   A good bit of the item stem is designed to give the test taker basic information on the novel should the test taker be unfamiliar with it. However, if you are unfamiliar with the novel, you will still be able to respond appropriately to the item. Notice that the question is about the *activity* that Mr. Allen has devised for the class. Sentence 5 specifies that the focus of the question is oral language—this should guide your selection of the response.

- Response A: It is very likely that some groups will examine our formal government documents in preparing their response to the assignment. However, citing evidence from these documents is more of a research and inquiry skill rather than an oral language skill.
- Response B: To respond effectively to the assignment, students will have to select evidence from the novel to persuade the school board audience. This response correlates with TEKS that require students to produce texts for oral presentation that demonstrate audience awareness.
- Response C: The class activity does not call for a formal debate. It may seem that the students are "debating" which character is in the right, but the scenario the teacher has set up is not a debating activity.
- Response D: While students will have to write a scripted speech, this is only part of the teacher's objectives. The fact that the "school board" will offer a decision at the end focuses the activity on the effectiveness of the evidence presented.

Response B best meets the specifications of the item stem.

## 8-12 Practice Item: Oral Language

(1) Ms. Blair's English III high school class is reading *Lord of the Flies* (Golding, 1959). (2) During each day's discussion of the previous night's reading, students have been arguing with each other about what some believe to be the unrealistic nature of the events that occur in the novel. (3) When one student asserts that "no one would ever act that way in real life," Ms. Blair decides to bring the events of the novel to life for the students. (4) To help students understand the characters' actions, she identifies pivotal scenes in the novel and allows students to work in groups to dramatize the events. (5) As each group presents its dramatization, the rest of the class will comment on the "actors'" performances to determine how effectively they act out the scenes. (6) This activity is most appropriate for meeting which of the following teaching goals?

    A. To provide an opportunity for students to analyze and interpret a literary text using verbal and nonverbal oral language communication strategies.

B. To prepare students for an essay on the topic, "Mankind is fundamentally savage; if you remove the trappings of civilization, we inexorably regress to savage behavior."

C. To encourage students to think carefully about the assertions they make during class discussions.

D. To help students identify with literary texts on a personal basis.

*Analysis.*   If this were an actual test item, it might be difficult to determine whether the item focuses on a literature teaching activity or on an oral language activity. In the context of TEKS, *dramatizations* of literary scenes are considered oral language (listening/speaking) activities rather than literature activities. Consequently, you should consider this item as one intended to test your understanding of oral language applications in the classroom.

- Response A: To construct a dramatization of the scene, students would have to analyze and interpret virtually every line of that passage in the novel. The performance would have to "translate" into drama every description provided in the scene as well as the dialogue included there.
- Response B: Writing an essay on a prompt about civilization and savagery seems an appropriate component for a unit on *Lord of the Flies*. This response focuses on a writing activity.
- Response C: While it is important for students to back up opinions using evidence, class discussions should foster a free exchange of ideas and should invite dialogue among students. Response C suggests that the teacher wants students to self-censor the questions they raise and the assertions they make, a situation not conducive to the practices associated with effective use of oral language in the classroom. Furthermore, it suggests that the assignment is punitive rather than instructional in nature.
- Response D: The dramatization is likely to enhance the students' engagement with the novel. Helping students identify with literary themes and events in the literary texts they read is an important aspect of the *literature* component of TEKS and educator standards. This practice item, however, is focused on oral language.

Response A best meets the specifications of the item stem.

## Analyzing Oral Language Items on the Sample Test

If you have identified the oral language items on your sample test, you should attempt those items at this point. Don't forget the response strategies presented in Test Prep Tip 6. Consciously use the information in TEKS, educator standards, and this chapter to guide your responses to the sample items.

---

REFLECTION FOR YOUR TExES JOURNAL:   Write about your sense of preparedness for the oral language portion of the TExES exam you will be taking. Having worked through this chapter, how confident do you feel about your grasp of the terms and concepts related to listening and speaking? Are there areas of oral language you still do not understand? What strategies will you use to guide your test preparation in oral language?

---

# Chapter Summary

- Oral language in the classroom incorporates listening and speaking processes.
- Oral language impacts virtually every aspect of ELA classroom interactions, but in the context of TExES, it is crucial that we consider oral language activities almost in isolation. In other words, although most test items that focus on oral language will integrate other language arts skills into the test item, we need to keep our attention on the particular oral language skill that the item mentions.
- Read some of the Selected Resources to fill in gaps in your understanding of oral language practices and pedagogy.

# Selected Resources: Oral Language

You should begin your review of resources in oral language by reading the chapters on this topic in the Comprehensive Resources listed in Chapter 1. In addition to explaining general principles governing oral communication as a discipline, most of those chapters also include descriptions of classroom activities designed to develop students' listening and speaking skills.

*A Prairie Home Companion with Garrison Keillor.* (2004). Minnesota Public Radio. Retrieved May 31, 2004 from http://prairiehome.publicradio.org
  The eclectic nature of Keillor's radio show makes it a good preparation resource for TExES candidates. Listening to even one show will help test takers recognize the oral language skills that are necessary to reach out to audiences via radio. Basically a humorous program, Keillor's show is likely to teach the TExES candidate much about audience awareness and about tailoring comments, pauses, inflections, and word choice to a listening audience. Neither TEKS nor educator standards specifically mention radio as a media literacy or oral language component, but radio continues to be an important communication and entertainment medium, and TExES candidates should be prepared to respond to questions about integrating radio into ELA instruction. Familiarity with the medium of radio will do much to develop the TExES candidate's understanding of the critical listening skills required for appreciating radio messages. Thus, it would be a good test preparation strategy to learn a bit about radio as an oral communication medium.

Burke, J. (2003). *The English teacher's companion: A complete guide to classroom, curriculum, and the profession* (2nd ed.). Portsmouth, NH: Heinemann.
> Chapter 8, Teaching Speaking and Listening: The Verbal Curriculum, provides a strong introduction to activities that fall into the realm of oral language instruction. The TExES candidate will find in this chapter many terms that occur in TEKS and educator standards on oral language. Burke defines, explains, and, in some cases, uses actual class activities to illustrate basic oral language terms.

Cooper, P. J., & Simonds, C. J. (2003). *Communication for the classroom teacher.* (7th ed.). Boston: Allyn and Bacon.
> This book includes chapters on many topics mentioned in TEKS and educator standards, including listening, verbal and nonverbal communication, small group communication, and storytelling. In addition, there are many sections within chapters that address topics relevant to TExES preparation, such as communication and cultural diversity, parent-teacher conferences, active listening, and gender and ethnicity in classroom communication.

Dickinson, D. K., McCabe, A., & Sprague, K. (2003). Teacher rating of oral language and literacy (TROLL): Individualizing early literacy instruction with a standards-based rating tool. *The Reading Teacher 56*(6), 554-564.
> Describes TROLL (Teacher Rating of Oral Language and Literacy), a measurement instrument developed by Dickinson to assess a young child's literacy development in oral language, reading, and writing. Although the article is highly technical, the TExES candidate can learn much about the way oral language development is manifested in the classroom. TROLL includes questions about the child's conversation skills, the way the child initiates exchanges about at-home experiences, the child's interest in oral reading activities, and many other aspects of literacy development. The TROLL tables included in the article area are useful for conceptualizing the things children do in classrooms that provide teachers important information about oral language, reading, and writing development.

Ellis, L., Gere, A. R., & Lamberton, L. J. (2003). Out loud: The common language of poetry. *English Journal 93*(1), 44-49.
> The authors suggest that because poetry is inherently oral, it should be taught as oral performance. The authors discuss a "slam poetry" application in their high school English classrooms in which students perform their own or other poets' poems using not only typical oral interpretation strategies but moving beyond that to literally using their whole bodies in the performance. The authors suggest that performance poetry can be a way of revitalizing students' interest in poetry. In the context of TEKS and educator standards, this article illustrates the value of incorporating oral interpretation of literature and other texts in the ELA classroom.

Goulden, N. R. (1998). Implementing speaking and listening standards: Information for English teachers. *English Journal 88*(1), 90-96.
> Offers a good overview of what oral language in the ELA classroom encompasses. Goulden defines many key terms and helps readers understand the role of oral language in the language arts curriculum. TExES candidates at all certification levels will find this article instructive and highly applicable to test preparation.

Johannessen, L. R. (2003). Strategies for initiating authentic discussion. *English Journal 93*(1), 73-79.
> Johannessen's premise is that students have difficulty engaging with literary texts because teachers spend more time talking about the texts then listening to what students have to say about those texts. Johannessen presents several activities designed to promote authentic discussion in the classroom, discussion in which students are genuinely engaged that promotes critical thinking skills that enhance learning in all language arts areas. TExES candidates will find value in the specific activities Johannessen presents, both in the context of teaching commonly taught literary texts, such as *Lord of the Flies* and "To Build a Fire" and in integrating current events and controversial issues into ELA teaching. Although this article is set in the context of a high school classroom, the information is relevant to elementary and middle school TExES preparation as well.

# 6 Media Literacy

When I introduce our media literacy unit to my teacher certification candidates, I usually begin with an account of my reaction to *The Sixth Sense*, the Bruce Willis movie, directed by M. Night Shyamalan (1999). Here's more or less what I share with my students:

> I walked out of the theater extremely angry at myself at the end of *The Sixth Sense*. I kept muttering, "How could I have missed all the clues?" I *noticed* all the clues—the Bruce Willis character sustained a massive gunshot wound but he "survived" with no apparent lingering effects; no one other than the little boy ever spoke to him; his wife ate her anniversary dinner alone *apparently* because he didn't bother to show up on time; his wife watched their wedding video over and over *apparently* when he was late getting home. I filled in all the gaps and quashed the niggling questions I had as I watched. And then, when the character realizes he himself is dead, I literally bopped myself on the head and said, "I should have figured it out—the clues were all there!" In other words, I watched the movie *uncritically*—I ignored the clues the writer and director embedded in the movie to enhance my movie viewing experience.

I watched this movie without attention to the subtext, to the clues, to the teasing on the part of the director and screenplay author. I did not *think* about what was going on in the movie. *Thinking* about a movie or commercial or TV program or billboard or photograph or other nonprint text as we view these types of texts is exactly what media literacy is all about. Media literacy suggests that critically "reading" a nonprint text is essential to understanding and interpreting the text. Being media literate means recognizing that images, text, special effects, music, camera angles, color, etc. have been used by the creator or "author" of a nonprint text to manipulate the viewer/audience, much the way textual effects and literary and rhetorical devices are used by writers to influence the reader.

In *The English Teacher's Companion* (2003), noted ELA educator Jim Burke invites us to think about the meaning of "reading" as we allow more and more types of "texts" into the realm of ELA (p. 318). Burke's observation, in part, explains the incorporation of *media literacy* into TEKS and TExES educator standards and competencies. At its most basic form, media literacy represents an attempt to recognize the impact media of all sorts have on students' lives and the realization by educators that media must be "read" in order to be understood and interpreted effectively. Clearly, however, the principles we use in teaching children to read (e.g., phonetic awareness, comprehension skills, word recognition strategies, prediction) do not apply to "reading" nonprint texts. Instead, we need to identify the ways we "read" photographs, movies, billboards, Web pages, advertisements, commercials, and other nonprint texts to help our students become media literate.

**A NOTE FOR EC-4 CANDIDATES:**   Interestingly, there are no EC-4 educator standards test competencies on media literacy, and the view/representing categories of TEKS do not occur until Grade 4 TEKS. While there are numerous references throughout the EC-4 documents to illustrations, maps, figures, and other graphics, those references occur in the context of helping children learn how to use information from graphics to support and augment an existing text.

## An Overview of Media Literacy

The term *media literacy* encompasses so many types of media that it is difficult to settle on a definition that incorporates everything suggested by the term. So, this definition, of necessity, is general and broad.

**MEDIA LITERACY: A WORKING DEFINITION**   Media literacy reflects the ability to adapt strategies and skills for understanding, interpreting, analyzing, and critiquing *written* texts to a variety of *nonprint texts*. Media literacy entails the application of critical literacy skills as we consider, interpret, and evaluate nonprint texts.

Examples of nonprint texts include the following:

- Movies (and everything that goes into creating and/or appreciating a well-constructed movie)
- Videos
- Television programming (including different program genres)
- Print and nonprint advertising
- Visual aspects of traditional newspapers (such as layout, font choices, political cartoons, comic strips, photo choices)
- Photographs
- Graphics, tables, charts, and illustrations incorporated into written texts
- Music, both as a support to visual media and as a medium that can be examined on its own
- Computer-based communication platforms (e.g., Internet sites, email, chatrooms, instant messages, databases, software, newsgroups, listservs)
- Billboard advertisements and messages

Whether we agree with the rationale behind the inclusion of media literacy in ELA is irrelevant—the decision has been made by our discipline, and our task is to be informed enough about media literacy to be successful on that component of the TExES. It might be helpful to recognize that media literacy has been relegated to English Language Arts, no doubt, because of the way that nonprint communication media utilize and adapt traditional elements of communication, such as audience, purpose, message, author/sender, rhetorical/presentation strategies, and manipulation of language.

Media literacy components of TEKS and educator standards give teachers responsibility for guiding students not only in interpreting a variety of media but also for *producing* media. Kim Martin Long (2002) describes, in an *English in Texas* article, the teacher's responsibility in becoming media literate. Long points out that the degree of familiarity or comfort with media literacy that the teacher demonstrates is vital to enhancing this aspect of our students' proficiency in language arts (p. 20). Prospective ELA teachers should interpret this comment as a call to make a concerted effort to acquire some degree of competence in understanding and teaching this aspect of ELA. Long's statement points to the importance of keeping students at the center of our media literacy efforts: We teach media literacy because it helps students become more intelligent, more critical, more competent users/consumers of media.

As prospective ELA teachers, you should not consider media literacy an end in itself; instead, media literacy should complement and enhance the existing ELA curriculum. Furthermore, media literacy should not be dismissed as a fad that can water down the "real" ELA curriculum; the abundant and ever-growing literature on media literacy cogently argues for its permanence in the ELA curriculum.

Although many of you have taken courses in technology applications, it is not likely that the broad range of areas included in media literacy has been covered comprehensively in your teacher prep program. This chapter will provide only rudimentary information on media literacy, so it would be a good idea to read some of the Selected Resources at the end of this chapter to ensure that, going into your TExES exam, you have more than a superficial understanding of this ELA area.

It might be helpful to "flesh out" the definition of media literacy by looking at one particularly effective *English Journal* article on media literacy. Writing about how she uses television to teach media literacy, E. Krueger (1998) writes, "Regardless of the 'text,' the themes of both literature and television are similar. . . . Using television in the English classroom provides students with another vehicle to construct meaning, to exercise critical thinking skills, and to evaluate the quality of a production" (p. 18). Krueger's article is particularly instructive for teachers who want to understand how media literacy can enhance students' understanding of traditional aspects of response to texts. She writes:

> In response to the first episode of "The Wonder Years," one student singled out the moment when Kevin and his parents, who had just left the principal's office where Kevin was severely reprimanded for misconduct, learn that their neighbor, Wayne Cooper, has been killed in Vietnam. The camera zooms in on Mr. Arnold's hand as it presses down on Kevin's shoulder. The students understand that it is the

camerawork that manipulates the audience's emotions so we feel deeply the loss of a young man who could have been one of the Arnold boys. Students have no problem articulating responses to coming-of-age issues in television shows. (p. 18)

Krueger's article provides a good introduction to media in the language arts classroom. She explains her rationale for incorporating media into her classes (we need to help students become critical consumers and users of media). In addition, this passage from her article calls our attention to the language we need to adopt when we work with visual texts. (This article provides a smattering of media literacy terminology [e.g., *zooming in, camera angles, high angle shot*] that we should use in presenting media texts in our classrooms.) Most of us insist that our students learn the language that they need in order to talk about literature and about writing. The same applies to helping our students become media literate: Students need to acquire the vocabulary that will help them discuss nonprint media with the facility that they discuss poetry, nonfiction texts, or their own writing. Krueger's article also includes discussions of specific activities that show how her students are able to analyze and produce media texts. If you have no preparation in media literacy, reading through Krueger's article will crystallize the way this ELA area can be turned into productive classroom activities.

---

REFLECTION FOR YOUR TExES JOURNAL:   Think of some of your most interesting experiences with nonprint media. What are your favorite movies? What criteria do you use for designating movies as your favorites? How about commercials—what aspects of commercials require more than casual attention?

---

# Coordinating TEKS, Educator Standards, and Test Competencies in Media Literacy

The term *media literacy* occurs in educator standards and in test competencies, but in TEKS, beginning with Grade 4, the concept is covered under the categories Viewing/representing/interpretation; Viewing/representing/analysis; and Viewing/representing/production (K-Grade 3 TEKS do not include these categories). Figure 6.1 shows you how to coordinate TEKS, educator standards, and test competencies in media literacy as you study for your TExES test level. Let's designate pink as our color code for this ELA area. Make sure you highlight and flag the TEKS and educator standards shown in Figure 6.1 in pink or whatever color you designate as your media literacy color code.

---

REFLECTION FOR YOUR TExES JOURNAL:   Jot down key terms and unknown terms from TEKS, educator standards, and sample test items in media literacy. Make sure you are able to define or apply all the terms you jotted down by the time you complete your TExES study in media literacy.

**FIGURE 6.1   Media Literacy Study Chart**

| EC-4 | | | |
| --- | --- | --- | --- |
| **TEKS K-4** | **Educator Standards** | **Test Competencies** | **Courses** |
| Viewing/representing/interpretation (Grade 4) Viewing/representing/analysis (Grade 4) Viewing/representing/production (Grade 4) | No media literacy standards | No media literacy competencies | Technology applications Communication/speech |

| 4-8 | | | |
| --- | --- | --- | --- |
| **TEKS Grades 4 and 5** **TEKS Middle School** | **Educator Standards** | **Test Competencies** | **Courses** |
| Viewing/representing/interpretation Viewing/representing/analysis Viewing/representing/production | Standard VII. Viewing and Representing | Competency 8 (Viewing and Representing) | Technology applications Communication/speech |

| 8-12 | | | |
| --- | --- | --- | --- |
| **TEKS Grade 8** **TEKS High School** | **Educator Standards** | **Test Competencies** | **Courses** |
| Viewing/representing/interpretation Viewing/representing/analysis Viewing/representing/production | Standard IX | Competency 011 | Technology applications Communication/speech |

# A Glossary of Selected Media Literacy Terms and Concepts

The terms in the glossary are defined and explained in the context of the viewing/representing TEKS and the media literacy educator standards and competencies. So, for example, while you may have a general understanding of the terms *advertising, movies,* or *billboards,* the explanation provided is designed to put the term in the context of TExES expectations.

**advertising:**   Television commercials, radio commercials, and print advertising. Students must be taught to "deconstruct" advertising, print and nonprint, by recognizing how images, color, type, language, persuasion strategies, narrative techniques, music, dialogue (or the absence of dialogue), and other elements of advertising contribute to the intended impact of an ad.

**billboards:**   A form of advertising that takes advantage of the time we spend in our cars. Billboards convey specific advertising messages as well as shape viewers' response to social and political issues. Attention should also be drawn to the layout of billboards: placement of images, use of color, use of text.

**computers in the classroom:**   Though an aspect of technology in the classroom, also a means of developing media literacy. The incorporation of computers into the language arts curriculum must include the ability to use the Internet wisely (in other words to be able to discriminate between reliable and questionable Web sites). As a function of media literacy, students are expected to use email, Web pages, databases, newsgroups, and listservs to enhance their language arts education.

**cropping:**   Editing a picture so that distracting or superfluous elements of the photograph are cut out of the final picture. Cropping enables a photographer to focus on a particular aspect of the picture and thereby influence the viewer's response to the photograph. Knowing that published images have been cropped is an important aspect of media literacy. The way a picture is cropped significantly impacts the message it conveys.

**data gathering techniques:**   Questionnaires, feedback forms, focus groups, interview questions, and other vehicles that can be used to collect data that can be incorporated into student-produced reports and projects. Students must be taught to develop data-gathering techniques that effectively target the intended audience and that include questions that will elicit the necessary data. While data-gathering techniques in themselves are not media literacy activities, the data that is gathered can be presented using a variety of nonprint media.

**design elements:**   Shape, lines, colors, texture, light, shadows, repetition, placement and arrangement of elements used in visual images.

**editing:**   The manipulation of elements of visual images. Students must understand that images in visual media are planned, posed, cropped, juxtaposed, colored, and shaded to manipulate the intended viewers' reactions. In other words, students need to know that through editing, images can be transformed from a straightforward visual representation into a rhetorical tool.

**illustrations (of written texts):**   Mostly applicable to young readers who, as part of literacy development, must learn how illustrations support a written text.

**integration of technology:**   Art, pictures, graphics, video, and music that authors and editors use to enhance and/or complement the reader's appreciation and understanding of a message. Throughout all TEKS categories at all levels, there is a recurring expectation that students should have opportunities to respond to literature, produce writing, and create projects through technology applications. While TEKS do not specify what those applications could be, we may reasonably assume that these include word processing, desktop publishing, video, and presentation programs such as PowerPoint, Internet resources, and visuals. Using technology effectively is an aspect of media literacy.

**literary elements in nonprint media:**   Symbols, analogies, irony, foreshadowing, allusions, conflict, and other traditional literary elements integrated into nonprint media through the use of color, light and shadow, text, camera angles, music, camera movement, background, framing, for example.

**logical fallacies in nonprint media:**   Overgeneralization, stereotyping, begging the question, red herrings, equivocation, nonsequiturs, and faulty analogy. Students should be guided to view television, movies, commercials, and other nonprint media with the awareness that fallacies frequently occur in all forms of media.

**maps, charts, graphs:**   Visual texts that require special decoding abilities. The ability to "read" maps, charts, and graphs is an element of literacy; because information is arranged visually as well as verbally, students must be taught how to decode the information in these graphics and as well as how to use such graphics effectively in texts they produce.

**media constructions of reality:**   The subtle and overt ways in which media shape viewers' responses to topics, events, and problems. Students should be led to recognize that news media, advertisers, and media companies do much to shape viewers' understanding of reality, whether it be a war in which the nation is engaged, attitudes toward specific groups, or attitudes toward aspects of society, government, or the environment. Above all, students must understand that media do not necessarily represent absolute "truth," that even newscasts are reflections and constructions of editorial decisions about what constitutes "news." The ELA teacher, according to SBEC and TEA, has a responsibility to help students understand how media contribute to constructing our view of reality.

**media presentations of culture:**  Media choices that contribute to viewers' and consumers' conceptions of particular groups, including specific cultures, ethnic groups, age groups, specific populations, gender, for example. A good exercise for showing students how to detect media presentations of culture is to watch television commercials. For the most part, commercials seem to reinforce stereotypes about gender, education, class, ethnicity, and age.

**movies:**  "Texts" to be analyzed and interpreted much the way we analyze and interpret literary texts. The media-literate student notices camera angles, the positioning of actors on the screen, the play between light and dark, the use of music, the cuts from scene to scene, background in important scenes, actors' reaction shots, and other strategies that define the craft of movie making. In addition, the literary devices we use to enhance our appreciation of literature have a place in movies as well. Students should be shown how to recognize symbols, metaphors, motifs, foreshadowing, satire, and other literary devices in movies.

**multimedia reports:**  Student presentations that utilize and incorporate media other than print, such as PowerPoint presentations, videos, movies, poster presentations, and photo portfolios. Students should be given frequent opportunities to demonstrate their ability to manipulate visual images in order to produce a specific effect on an audience or to enhance the message of the presentation.

**music:**  An important aspect of much nonprint media. Think, for example, of how many commercials rely on music and visuals only, no dialogue. Think also of how important a movie score or soundtrack is in helping us understand the action, emotions, and foreshadowing within the narrative of the movie. Students should be given multiple opportunities to incorporate music into technology presentations and teachers should enhance lessons in literature and other language arts areas by appropriately integrating music.

**newspapers in the classroom:**  Although technically a print medium, much newspaper "text" is nonprint, e.g., comic strips, political cartoons, layout, advertising, type fonts and sizes, color, and photographs. Understanding that these visual elements represent choices made by editors and/or writers enables students to read all aspects of newspapers effectively and intelligently.

**nonprint texts:**  Television programs, photographs, Web sites, email, billboards, television and magazine advertising, movies, videos, music, and political cartoons. These are viewed as "texts" when traditional elements of print texts (e.g., message, genre, sender/writer, receiver/listener/reader, style, voice, audience awareness, rhetorical strategies, persuasive appeals, language choices) are used in analyzing, interpreting, and evaluating such texts.

**persuasive strategies:**  The application of traditional strategies of persuasion to the interpretation of nonprint media. An understanding of the classical appeals—emotional, logical, and ethical—should be part of students' strategies for understanding and analyzing nonprint media. Particularly in television commercials, appeals are a vital part of the impact of the commercial, and students should be taught to recognize how these appeals are manifested in nonprint texts.

**photographs:**  A form of visual composition. Photographs are far more than fixed, "truthful" images of events, persons, or sites. Students need to recognize that a photograph represents choices made by photographers starting from when the image is framed in the viewfinder, moving through effects integrated during the developing or printing process, and ending with an artifact that is displayed or published. Students should understand that photographic images are manipulated by the photographer and editor to produce a desired effect upon viewers. Students should be aware of how such elements as cropping, shadows, light, color, filters, focus, placement of elements in the photograph, background, and facial expressions influence the viewer. Furthermore, students should be given opportunities to study famous photographs that illustrate the artistic, social, historical, political, and personal impact of photography.

**radio:**  A means of integrating oral language *and* media literacy into the ELA curriculum. Preparing and staging mock radio broadcasts enables students to think about audience, content, rhetoric, delivery, and presentation in ways that are different from preparation of a traditional speech or a written essay. Students should be taught that radio continues to have a very strong presence in American culture, that radio is used for much more than playing the week's top 50 hits. Listening to and analyzing the effectiveness of well-known radio programs, talk radio programs, radio news programs, and personality-specific radio programs should help students understand much about the impact of radio in modern society.

**sound techniques:**   The manipulation of aspects of sound in producing a video or movie. In analyzing and producing videos and movies, students must have some understanding of how a message, story, or purpose can be conveyed through sound (e.g., intensity, background music, clarity of dialogue, voiceovers, soundtrack, sound effects, or silence).

**technology presentations:**   Reports and/or presentations that require the teacher's and students' ability to use technology (e.g., computers, Internet resources, video production) to enhance teaching and learning.

**television genres:**   Documentaries, news broadcasts, news magazines, sitcoms, dramas, reality shows, for example. Students should be guided toward understanding that each TV genre must be viewed with an awareness of the "rules" that govern it. In addition, students should be provided with opportunities to stage mock television programs to demonstrate their understanding of how this medium works.

**video segments:**   Short clips of any video (for example, a movie, a commercial, or a documentary) used to teach a language arts concept (such as irony, audience awareness, rhetorical strategies, or use of light and shadows).

**visual images:**   Pictures, text art, designs, layout, and color that contribute to the meaning of a visual text.

**visual techniques:**   Camera angles, light/shadow interplay, zooming in/out, close-ups, field of view, framing, background, panning, wide angle shots, reaction shots, sequencing, special effects, and lighting. In analyzing and producing videos and movies, students must have some understanding of how a message, story, or purpose can be conveyed through visual techniques.

**Web pages:**   A type of visual text that integrates print as well as graphics to create a message. Students should understand that Web pages can manipulate the viewer/reader's response through word choice, syntax, color, automatic links, and other devices. Although some expertise is required to compose an effective Web page, students should be given the opportunity to use and create Web pages that support the language arts curriculum.

## Classroom Practices: Media Literacy

In teaching media literacy, the ELA teacher should demonstrate proficiency in the following instructional skills and competencies:

- Helping students see connections between nonprint texts and traditional literary texts.
- Knowing how to use all aspects of word processing programs and other computer programs to help students make their texts visually and technically effective.
- Knowing what media students are currently interested in by reading magazines, watching television programs, viewing movies, and listening to albums or CDs that appeal to students.
- Recognizing the importance of helping students understand and interpret nonprint texts so that they may become intelligent, critical users of media.
- Helping students understand that analyzing nonprint texts can enhance their enjoyment of popular media.

- Providing opportunities for students to enhance their understanding of language arts by producing a variety of nonprint texts.
- Incorporating a variety of nonprint texts in the teaching of language arts.
- Understanding that strategies for reading, interpreting, and analyzing literary texts can be adapted to the study of nonprint texts.

---

REFLECTION FOR YOUR TEXES JOURNAL: In what ways have your teachers and professors incorporated media literacy activities into your language arts instruction? What media literacy classroom activities do you recall as being particularly effective?

---

# Test Item Exercises

The items in this section are designed to help you apply your understanding of the terms, concepts, and principles we discussed in this chapter in scenarios that focus on media literacy.

## EC-4 Practice: Media Literacy

(1) A third-grade teacher wants to develop her students' ability to recognize that animated features and movies have a structure that enables viewers to appreciate and understand the story conveyed by the film. (2) Students will be watching the film *Harry Potter and the Sorcerer's Stone* (Columbus, 2001) to fulfill this objective. (3) Which of the following activities would best help students begin to understand the structure of movies?

A. Students are assigned several chapters in J. K. Rowlings' novel, *Harry Potter and the Sorcerer's Stone* (1997), and then they watch the movie scenes that portray the events in those chapters.
B. Students watch the opening scenes of the movie and fill out storyboards in which they represent the actions and problems portrayed in each scene.
C. Students watch the entire movie and then, in groups, prepare and stage an "epilogue" scene that moves beyond the ending of the movie.
D. The teacher distributes a T-chart to students labeled "book" in one column and "movie" in the other. Students enter differences they see between the book and the movie as they watch the movie.

*Analysis.* The item stem clearly establishes that this is a media literacy item—the activity at the core of the item is viewing a movie to fulfill a specific objective: to help students realize that movies have structure (just as stories have plot elements).

- Response A: Viewing the movie in increments following the reading of relevant chapters would be a good activity to help students see the changes that are necessary in transforming a written text into a movie—which is a different objective from the one specified in the stem.

- Response B: A storyboard is a traditional literacy development activity used in understanding the elements of a story plot. The advantage of using this activity would be that students would already be familiar with how a storyboard contributes to the reader's understanding of a story. Adapting the strategy to movie scenes would be a first step in helping students realize that in movies, scenes are used to segment the story into units that both sequentially and collectively complete the whole story.
- Response C: This post-viewing activity would be useful for determining the students' level of comprehension of the whole movie. In order to successfully complete this activity, students would have to have fundamental knowledge of how to "read" a movie. In other words, this is a higher level activity than what the stem specifies.
- Response D: Recognizing the differences between a book and the movie adaptation is an important aspect of media literacy, but this is not the objective specified by the stem.

Response B best fits the specifications of the prompt.

## 4-8 Practice: Media Literacy

(1) A teacher of middle schoolers wants to help students identify the strategies used to present national news on television. (2) As a beginning activity, the teacher has the students watch a 5-minute segment of a national newscast. (3) After the segment, the teacher leads students in a whole class discussion in which they identify everything other than the "reading of the news" that contributed to the presentation of the news during the segment. (4) Then, the teacher goes to the back of the classroom, with the students facing forward, and reads a transcript of a different 2-minute segment of a national televised news program. (5) The teacher then asks the class, "In what ways is *listening* to television news different from *watching* the news on television?" (6) This activity might best promote students' understanding of which of the following aspects media literacy?

A. Students draw preliminary conclusions about the way that screen graphics, video clips, and other visual elements contribute to television news reports.
B. Students realize that attentive listening is critical in understanding television news reports.
C. Students understand the difference between news presented by a television news anchor and news heard over the radio.
D. Students explore the ways that newscasters' tone, gestures, and body language influences the viewers' perception of news.

*Analysis.* The sentences of the item stem include several important qualifications and specifications: The teacher is focusing on television news reports; this is a *beginning* activity; the teacher is using two related activities to reinforce the point he or she wants to make.

- Response A: Given the initial activity (students watching and commenting on a short segment of television news), the follow-up activity seems designed to help students focus on visual elements incorporated into television news reporting.
- Response B: If the teacher were focusing on oral language, this would be an appropriate response, but the item stem places the questions in the realm of media literacy. Furthermore, the activity is designed to focus students' attention on everything other than the actual reading of the news.
- Response C: The radio connection is not established in the item stem.
- Response D: This would be an appropriate class discussion in a later unit on the way media influence viewers' perceptions of news events. The stem, however, specifies that the activity described is a *beginning* activity.

Response A best meets the specifications of the item stem.

## 8-12 Practice: Media Literacy

(1) Following a three-week unit on movies, a high school ELA teacher wants to promote her students' abilities to create a media project that demonstrates their understanding of how visual elements (such as camera angles, reaction shots, background, zooming in, light and shadow) contribute to the viewer's construction of meaning. (2) Which of the following activities would best achieve this teaching goal?

A. Reading several published critiques of *Citizen Kane* (Welles, 1941) and identifying the strategies that director Orson Welles introduced in this ground-breaking movie.
B. Assigning a collaborative project in which students create video presentations of a specific scene in a story or novel the class has recently discussed.
C. Writing an essay that analyzes the video techniques implemented in a recent Best Picture Academy Award-winning movie.
D. Watching the directors' comments on DVDs of several award-winning movies and discussing what they believe are the most effective choices each director made in the production of the movies.

*Analysis.* If you have studied at least one grade level TEKS in the 8-12 level, you are aware that the *production* of media projects is included in the media literacy categories. This item stem specifies that the teacher wants to address the *production* of media projects, and this is the qualifier that should guide your response choice.

- Response A: This response draws on the long-standing recognition of Orson Welles' *Citizen Kane* as a movie that introduced innovative effects and approaches. The Response A activity would allow students to join in the conversation of movie production and to learn terms and to see how cinematic effects and principles are utilized in this movie. It would be a good activity for *preparing* students to carry out the teaching objective.

- Response B: This activity calls for students to *create* a visual text. Even if the video production is limited to a scene from a story or novel, students would have to make use of the video strategies specified in the item stem.
- Response C: Writing an essay requires critical thinking about the subject, and the teacher would be able to determine whether students can recognize the stipulated visual effects in a specific movie. However, it is a writing rather than media literacy activity.
- Response D: Listening to directors discuss the visual effects they've incorporated into movies and the rationale behind them would be instructive to students. It would provide an opportunity for students to "get inside" a director's mind and understand how and why visual effects are chosen. This would be a good activity to implement earlier in the three-week unit, when students are acquiring familiarity with video techniques.

Response B best meets the specifications of the prompt.

## Study Strategies for Media Literacy

Because media literacy is probably the one area you have not covered thoroughly and systematically in your teacher prep courses, you might have to prepare for this portion of the test a bit differently from the other areas.

- In general, try to become more aware of how television commercials, movies, billboards, and the other nonprint texts mentioned in this chapter utilize visual strategies to engage and influence the viewer.
- Read some of the materials included in the resource list at the end of this chapter, particularly the articles from the National Council of Teachers of English journals. These articles are included in the resources chapter because they "operationalize" the implementation of media literarcy in the classroom. You will pick up new vocabulary, you will see a diversity of approaches for integrating media literacy in the ELA curriculum, and you will read explanations of how media knowledge contributes to students' proficiency in other language arts. Another good choice is reading the transcripts for *American Photography: A Century of Images* (1999) available on the PBS Web site. These transcripts offer valuable insights into the power and art of photography.
- Watch some classic movies (*Citizen Kane* is a good choice) and focus on how much of your construction of meaning is influenced by visual elements. If your library has a copy of the book produced for PBS's *American Photography* (see Selected Resources at the end of this chapter), spend some time looking at the photographs and reading what the authors have to say about the impact of photography on U.S. culture, politics, history, and social climate.
- Watch television commercials with a critical eye. Pay attention to how they exploit stereotypes, how music is incorporated into the commercial, and how literary techniques are adapted to the commercial.

- Pay attention to Web sites you visit, noticing how visual elements are used to influence your response to the pages.

## Analyzing Media Literacy Items on the Sample Test

The sample tests in the TExES preparation manuals include only a few media literacy items, but you should analyze these items carefully and completely, especially if you have had no formal training in media literacy. This chapter should provide sufficient background in this new language arts category to enable you to figure out the responses both to sample items and to actual test items.

---

REFLECTION FOR YOUR TExES JOURNAL: Assess your level of preparedness for attempting the media literacy segment of your TExES exam. Do you feel you have a good understanding of this new language arts area? Can you envision how you might integrate media literacy into language arts teaching? What study plans do you have in the area of media literacy as you continue your TExES preparation?

---

## Chapter Summary

- Media literacy is a relatively recent addition to the realm of English language arts. Make sure you have a firm understanding of what is meant by media literacy and what skills and activities reflect this new literacy.
- If you have no background in media literacy, read some of the resources suggested in this chapter to build up your understanding of this important ELA area.
- Try to become aware of your own media literacy as you "read" the nonprint texts that you encounter each day.

## Selected Resources: Media Literacy

Alvermann, D. E., & Xu, S. H. (2003). Children's everyday literacies: Intersections of popular culture and language arts instruction. *Language Arts 81*(2), 145-154.

> The authors' approach to using popular culture in the ELA classroom includes recognizing the importance of television, movies, video games, and computers in children's lives and using that interest to help them develop critical attitudes about popular culture without destroying the enjoyment they derive from those interests. The article includes discussion of numerous classroom activities in which popular culture "texts" (Los Cumbia Kings music, media coverage of Brittney Spears, Pokémon, Spider-Man, *Survivor*) are integrated into language arts instruction; the "texts" become a point of departure for developing students' critical literacy, which involves asking themselves questions about what they are "reading" visually, about what ideas and standards are suggested by these texts, and about how they can connect the worlds of music, television, video games, and popular movies to their own lives. While the article focuses on elementary level teaching, the approaches can be easily adapted to all teaching levels. An important aspect of Alvermann's and Xu's

argument for including popular culture in the ELA classroom is their insistence that teachers learn what their students are watching and playing at home so that those literacies can be utilized to enhance traditional literacy.

*American photography: A century of images.* (1999). Public Broadcasting Service. Retrieved May 15, 2003 from http://www.pbs.org/ktca/americanphotography/filmandmore/index.html
> This Web version of the PBS documentary offers a quick, entertaining, and highly informative introduction to the impact of photography in shaping America's national image. The narrator discusses "classic" American photographs as well as categories of photography.

Brooks, J. (1998). Teenagers evaluating modern media. *English Journal 87*(1), 21-33.
> Brooks asserts that students' interest in nonprint media should be used to develop their analytical skills for evaluating movies, CDs, television programs, music videos, computer programs, and other nonprint texts. Probably the most valuable element of this article is Brooks's set of questions that can be distributed to students to help them analyze movies, music videos, television programs, computer programs, CDs, and even live performances. The questions that Brooks crafts actually can help the TExES candidate who has had no training in media literacy understand how this ELA component can be worked into a traditional language arts curriculum. Even more significant for the TExES candidates is Brooks's connections between nonprint texts and traditional literary texts: He shows how he helps students understand that analyzing texts such as music and videos requires the same sort of critical thinking skills that they apply in analyzing literature.

Field, S. (1982). *Screenplay: The foundations of screenwriting.* New York: Dell.
> It is probably unrealistic to expect the TExES candidate to review a work as specialized as this one, but even skimming through one or two chapters will contribute significantly to the candidate's understanding of what makes movies technically "good." This book also provides the vocabulary we need when we talk critically about movies (such as *plot point, sequence, scene, character, camera angles, background*). Discussion of the technical aspects of many well-known movies, including *Chinatown* and *Citizen Kane,* enable TExES candidates to understand TEKS and educator standards that call for helping students analyze and produce visual texts.

Goldberg, V., & Silberman, R. (1999) *American photography: A century of images.* San Francisco: Chronicle Books.
> The companion book to the PBS Web site, this book offers valuable information on the technical and aesthetic aspects of photographs. It also helps us understand the role that photography has had in shaping our national image. Famous photographs are analyzed from the photographer's point of view, from the cultural or societal impact they have had, and from the viewer's perspective. This book truly helps the test candidate understand the TEKS statements in the viewing/representing categories about the messages conveyed by photographs.

Krueger, E. (1998). Media literacy does work, trust me. *English Journal 87*(1), 17-20.
> For the TExES candidate, this article is valuable because of the author's application of terms and activities associated with analysis of literary texts to analysis of visual texts, particularly television and movies. Krueger organizes her article on the basis of National Council of Teachers of English guidelines for media literacy instruction and provides specific, clearly explained classroom applications of each guideline. Krueger's discussion includes adaptations of traditional literature teaching activities (such as reader response journals, discussions of theme, understanding of genre constraints and expectations, character development, culture) in the context of media texts. She discusses classroom activities involving *The Wonder Years, What's Eating Gilbert Grape,* and *The Godfather.* In addition, the inclusion of terms related to video production (e.g., *high angle shots, zooming in, cinematic techniques*) makes this an instructional article for the TExES candidate with little exposure to media literacy.

Lund, D. J. (1998). Video production in the English language arts classroom. *English Journal 87*(1), 78-82.

Recognizing that many ELA teachers lack technical knowledge to help students produce videos, Lund provides a list of resources for teachers to educate themselves in video production and also demonstrates how traditional ELA and teaching skills can be adapted to help students successfully produce videos. TExES candidates should be aware that TEKS and educator standards that refer to helping students produce videos suggest that video production could be the focus of some test items; thus, becoming at least minimally educated about the technology and language of video production should be part of the TExES candidate's preparation.

Martin, J. L. (2002). Tights vs. tattoos: Filmic interpretations of Romeo and Juliet. *English Journal* 92(1), 41-46.

Martin compares two movie versions of *Romeo and Juliet* (Zeffirelli's 1968 version and Luhrmann's 1996 version) in the context of the technical differences between the two productions. Martin clearly demonstrates that the elements of production distinct to each version contribute to shaping profoundly different understandings of the story. This article is particularly helpful for TExES preparation in media literacy because of the author's facility in using and applying technical terms related to movie production. The TEKS category viewing/representing/producing includes terms that are quite technical and that might intimidate the test taker who has had no classroom exposure to media literacy terms and concepts. While Martin's purpose is not to educate the reader in cinematic terms and practices, we do in fact learn a lot about movie production and about how directorial choices shape the viewer's response. Martin reminds us that it is important to give students the vocabulary they need to discuss and evaluate the genre of film, and she convincingly demonstrates that such discussion develops their critical thinking skills. This article will clarify much about media literacy for the TExES candidate who has had no exposure to this new language arts category.

Orfanella, L. (1998). Radio: The intimate medium. *English Journal 87*(1), 53-55.

The writer suggests that radio is an unappreciated medium, but then observes that its omnipresence in our lives makes radio an "intimate" medium; thus, students should be taught to understand how radio impacts their lives. Orfanella describes eight classroom activities that students can engage in to sharpen their understanding of radio.

Ostrow, J. (2003). A letter to a niece: Critical media literacy, one child at a time. *Voices from the Middle 10*(3), 23-27.

Although Ostrow frames the article in a conversation with and letter to her 12-year-old niece, she points to important considerations we should keep in mind about media literacy in our ELA classrooms. She argues that we should help students examine media critically by teaching them to ask themselves questions about the media they view and consume. Specifically, Ostrow is concerned about stereotypes promoted by visual media. However, she also points out that media convey messages about values and lifestyles that students should be taught to recognize and evaluate. Ostrow's letter to her niece offers prospective ELA teachers points to consider in integrating media into the classroom. While TEKS and educator standards include student and teacher expectations about media literacy, they do not suggest the problems and controversies raised by including this new language art into our traditional curriculum. Ostrow adeptly points us toward those controversies and gives us general questions to consider as we work media literacy into our ELA classrooms.

Pailliotet, A. W., Ladislaus, S., Rodenberg, R. K., Giles, J. K., & Macaul, S. L. (2000). Intermediality: Bridge to critical media literacy. *The Reading Teacher 54*(2), 208-219.

This article does much to explain the complexity of media literacy. Intermediality, according to the authors, is a term that allows us to examine the extensions of traditional literacy skills to a vast variety of nonprint texts, including television, movies, the Internet, body language, and advertising. In other words, media literacy does not require acquisition of a new body of literacy skills; instead, critical media literacy involves recognizing the intermediality of print and nonprint texts. To develop critical media literacy, students must recognize connections between the literacy skills they use in constructing meaning in print texts to constructing meaning in nonprint texts. The article includes descriptions of nine intermediality learning experiences that illustrate how students can be guided to use existing literacy competencies to analyze nonprint texts. Each activity clearly shows how specific literacy skills we usually associate with print literacy (such as experiential knowledge, genre knowledge, semantic maps, schema, scaffolding, and socialization) can be applied to analysis of nonprint texts. TExES candidates will find in this article classroom applications of many terms and concepts that appear but are not explained in TEKS and educator standards in the areas of viewing/representing (media literacy). This article is more challenging than most of the entries included as resources in this chapter, but it is well worth the effort involved. Upon reading this article, TExES candidates will understand not only *that* media literacy is a new component of ELA but *why* media literacy has been so easily and completely absorbed into language arts.

Phillips, W. H. (2005). *Film: An introduction* (3rd ed.). Boston: Bedford St. Martins.
Phillips' discussion of film is a valuable resource for TExES candidates who have had no coursework in film criticism. Terms associated with analysis of film are defined and thoroughly illustrated. Phillips uses a wide variety of films to support his comments, including many movies that can be incorporated into K-12 language arts classrooms.

Skretta, J. (1997). Beavis and Butt-head: Two more white males for the canon. *English Journal*, *86*(8) 24-28.
Skretta argues valiantly and persuasively for including pop icons Beavis and Butt-head in the canon, explaining that teachers can use students' familiarity with television and video texts as springboards for strengthening their understanding of literary elements, text structures, and significant literary themes. Skretta's article necessarily deals with negotiating parental cooperation in introducing a controversial text into the curriculum, albeit a nonprint text. Skretta's incorporation of Beavis and Butt-head into the traditional ELA curriculum includes research on attitudes toward the animated feature, discussion of social issues raised by the controversial nature of the show (such as a ratings system for television programs), analyzing literary elements utilized in the episodes, producing culminating projects that provide options for students to demonstrate their engagement with the Beavis and Butt-head unit. Skretta concludes by reminding us of our responsibility as ELA teachers to guide students toward becoming critical consumers of nonprint media. For the TExES candidate, this article should crystallize the place of media literacy in the language arts curriculum. It could be seen as an extreme application of media literacy, but Skretta's arguments for teaching Beavis and Butt-head along with Shakespeare echo prevailing attitudes about the importance of media literacy instruction. Finally, what Skretta writes about Beavis and Butt-head is applicable to any other nonprint text that appeals to our students and that has secured a fixed position in popular culture, such as Pokémon, MTV, anime, and numerous animated television shows and movies.

Vasquez, V. (2003). What Pokémon can teach us about learning and literacy. *Language Arts 81*(2), 118-125.
This is a "must read" article for any TExES candidate who harbors reservations about integrating popular culture into the language arts classroom or who doesn't quite see the rationale for using popular media to support literacy instruction. Vasquez suggests that children's ability to participate in the extensive world of Pokémon involves complex literacy skills as they learn to negotiate the many aspects of this fantasy world that involves the television series, movies, toys, trading card communities, and Internet sites. Vasquez's discussion of how she herself gradually developed the vocabulary, the thinking skills, the experiential knowledge, and the socialization required to participate in the Pokémon world illustrates what children must go through to develop the literacy skills we value in our ELA classrooms. Furthermore, Vasquez shows how the traditional reading skills and competencies we present in our classrooms are prerequisites for entering and remaining viable in the Pokémon world. Vasquez closes by urging us to recognize that children are developing the very literacy skills and attitudes toward reading that we struggle to teach them in the classroom in contexts that they themselves select, such as the Pokémon world.

# CHAPTER

# 7

# Pedagogical Practices

## Diversity, Technology, and Assessment

In this chapter, we will examine aspects of teaching that are germane to all disciplines, not just to English language arts: assessment, diversity, and technology. In literature devoted to theory and practice in language arts and other teaching areas, these are "hot topics." In classroom situations, issues of diversity, technology, and assessment can be troubling and frequently require adjustments to our teaching philosophies and teaching approaches.

In the context of test preparation, it is important to know how the terms in this chapter will establish parameters in objective item stems. For example, when incorporated into item stems, phrases such as "a student with *writing difficulties*" or "an English Language Learner" significantly impact the tenor of the item and should sharply focus your analysis of the possible responses to that item.

This chapter will offer definitions, explanations, and suggested resources for the following areas of English language arts pedagogy:

- Diversity
- Equity
- Technology applications
- Socialization
- Assessment
- Parental involvement

## TEKS and Educator Standards

You need to review the TEKS and educator standards for your certification level to identify the statements relevant to the topics we'll examine in this chapter. There are no separate TEKS on assessment, diversity, technology, or parental involvement. However, there are statements throughout all TEKS categories and educator standards about technology applications. Assessment, diversity, and parental involvement are the province of the teacher, so expectations about these pedagogical concerns are found throughout educator standards and skills and knowledge statements. Each certification level has an educator standard devoted to assessment. In addition, each educator standard includes knowledge or application statements that address assessment, and many of the ELA educator standards include statements about using technology to support and develop students' literacy skills. You should take time now to identify these standards and highlight them or flag them in violet, our color code for general pedagogical practices. In addition, you should review your grade level TEKS once more to identify references to technology, diversity, and assessment. Mark these in our violet color code.

---

**REFLECTION FOR YOUR TExES JOURNAL:**    As you work through TEKS and educator standards to identify statements related to diversity, assessment, technology, and parental involvement, jot down terms and phrases that seem particularly significant or that you do not understand. Make sure you are able to explain each of these terms by the time you work through the information in this chapter.

---

## A Glossary of Selected Terms in General Pedagogy

**assessment:**    Methods and strategies a teacher uses to determine whether students are meeting learning objectives and/or curricular expectations. Assessment can be used to monitor student achievement and to measure student progress. *Authentic assessment* calls for integration of assessment practices into day-to-day teaching as opposed to implementing an assessment at the end of a teaching unit. Discussions of student achievement increasingly avoid the use of the term "testing," possibly because of the negative associations conjured up by the idea of testing: for example, test anxiety, pass rates, student failure, and standardized testing. Instead, we now talk about "assessment," and we work at devising assessment methods that help us determine what and how our students are learning.

**authentic assessment:**    An approach to assessment that embeds assessment practices into teaching activities and uses assessment to promote student learning. Authentic assessment practices move away from traditional testing (end-of-unit objective tests, for example) partly because such testing frequently shows what the learner does not know rather than what the learner knows. Furthermore, traditional tests create anxiety in the learner, a situation that does not permit the learner to fully demonstrate his or her competence. In contrast, authentic assessment practices permit learners to demonstrate their knowledge and understanding of the topic under discussion.

**collaborative learning:**    Learning situations and activities in which students work in groups rather than individually. Collaborative learning, however, is much more than "group work." Ideally, in collaborative learning, students learn from and with each other; one learner's insights enable other learners to increase their own understanding of the subject. Collaborative learning situations help students develop socialization skills that are vital to negotiating learning. For example, a student who might be reluctant to ask a question in the context of a whole class discussion might feel comfortable raising the question in a small group setting. Collaborative learning, however, can also occur in a whole class setting. Teacher-led discussions in which students are encouraged to ask questions not just of the teacher but of each other, in which students' comments are valued and no response is diminished or ridiculed also help students learn collaboratively.

**cooperative learning:**    A feature of *collaborative learning*. In order to learn collaboratively, we must be able to negotiate with other learners as everyone works through the subject under discussion. Cooperative learning involves active listening, productive questioning, turn-taking, accepting responsibility—the skills that make us productive members of social groups. For cooperative learning to occur, teachers need to establish guidelines for group work and class discussions so that a few students do not monopolize the discussion or take over the bulk of the assigned work and quiet students do not fade into the background.

**culture:**    A difficult term to define, but usually refers to the beliefs, assumptions, behaviors, lifestyles, associations, and/or ethnic connections that shape an individual's view of the world. In the context of teaching, culture refers to several things. On one hand, the student's culture is an important part of his or her identity. But culture does not simply refer to ethnicity. Culture can be anything in the learner's background that shapes his or her construction of reality. Being aware of how a learner's culture impacts learning is an important part of teaching, and such awareness obviously calls for sensitivity to cultural differences on the part of the teacher. On a broader scale, the term "culture" suggests characteristics, practices, beliefs, views, and styles that we associate with ethnic, national, or religious groups of people, so we talk about Hispanic culture, Jewish culture, or Native American culture. Multicultural practices in teaching promote understanding and appreciation of other cultures.

**diversity:**    The acknowledgment and celebration of difference in learners. Difference may be socioeconomic, cultural, ethnic, gender-related, language-related, learning style–related, or developmental. The aim in recognizing and appreciating diversity is to make each learner feel special, understood, appreciated, and equal to all other learners. Recognition of diversity is a means of creating a classroom community in which equity reigns and every learner has equal access to information and to class activities that promote learning.

**English Language Learner:**    A student who is working toward acquiring competence in English. The ELL student may be an English as a Second Language learner, a bilingual student, or perhaps even a student who developmentally is somewhat behind the average learner at his or her grade level. Typically, however, the term ELL refers to students whose first language or home language is not English and thus require special attention so that they can understand and participate in classroom learning activities. English Language Learners may have difficulties receiving parental support for their academic activities since the parents may themselves have significant difficulties in English communication.

**ethnicity/ethnic diversity:**    Aspects of an individual's identity that are to some extent attributable to ethnic background. Recognition of and sensitivity about ethnic diversity is an important aspect of teaching. There is the assumption that all students will be treated equitably regardless of ethnic background. In some cases, this means understanding that some classroom behaviors and responses can be traced to ethnic traditions or expectations. However, in appropriate circumstances, the celebration and showcasing of difference is an important aspect of learning experiences. TEKS related to reading/culture focus on helping students recognize connections between their own and other cultures, and seeing those connections requires both recognizing difference and finding commonalities among ethnic groups and cultures.

**family/parental involvement:**    The inclusion of family members in the responsibilities of teaching and learning. Educator standards include numerous statements about collaboration with families to promote children's language arts competencies. In this context, literacy learning is a family event, with the family supporting the child's growing competence in the language arts and the teacher maintaining close contact with the family in order to foster continuing literacy growth. For English Language Learners, however, family support may be limited because of the lack of a literacy-rich environment, and the teacher must make adjustments in traditional outreach methods in order to involve ELL families as much as possible in the child's literacy development.

**formative evaluation:**   The feedback and guidance a teacher offers a learner during the process of completing a learning task. The teacher evaluates the learner's effort and evidence of progress at a particular point in the learning process, but does not assign a final, unchangeable grade. Instead, because the task is still in progress, the learner has the opportunity to improve the outcome as a result of the teacher's formative comments. For example, formative evaluation occurs in the writing process when a teacher looks over a draft and helps the writer figure out what areas should be improved. Formative evaluation is aimed at fostering a degree of independence in the learner, with the teacher pointing out strengths and weaknesses and the learner taking the initiative to work at reducing weaknesses and showcasing strengths.

**gender equity:**   In the context of teaching, the equal treatment of male and female students. Unfortunately, no statements about gender equity occur in TEKS or educator standards. However, ELA literature on teaching practices includes a significant discussion on gender equity. Because boys and girls so often react and respond quite differently in classroom situations, teachers must be aware of the sources or explanations for these different reactions and should work toward fostering a classroom community in which male and female students are treated equally, given equal amounts of attention, and considered equally capable of attaining teaching and learning goals.

**learning difficulties:**   In the context of TExES preparation, a specific problem or set of problems that causes a learner to function at a level below average or the norm established by other learners in the classroom. In an objective item stem, this should be a clue that the response must deflect attention from the traditional approach in a particular teaching situation toward the student's learning difficulties. This term is not likely to refer to the types of difficulties that a special education teacher or an educational diagnostician would handle. In the context of ELA/Reading TExES exams, learning difficulties suggest that a student needs specialized attention to overcome or cope with relatively minor weaknesses that prevent him or her from keeping up with classroom instruction and from making progress in specific instructional areas.

**socialization:**   Conversations, interactions, and other contacts among members of a community of learners. Students must be able to work with each other and with the teacher in a social setting that invites talk, questioning, negotiation, and gradual creation of understanding in the areas of language arts. Socialization is a necessary part of construction of meaning in all areas of language arts; for example, listening to what other readers have to say about a text is an important part of shaping our own understanding of that text. A teacher who recognizes the value of socialization encourages student talk and guides students in learning how to use classroom talk productively to shape their understanding of the topics and texts addressed in the classroom.

**student-centered:**   Instruction that focuses on the learner rather than on the curriculum or the teacher. In a teacher-centered classroom, the teacher is the dispenser of knowledge; the teacher sits figuratively and actually behind the desk; the students perform tasks assigned and directed by the teacher. In a student-centered classroom, the learners' needs are taken into account and in many cases shape instruction. While the teacher must, to some extent, function as the authority in the classroom, in a student-centered environment, the teacher provides many opportunities for learners to express their needs, adjusts the curriculum to meet those needs, and strives to create a community of learners in which both students and teacher can learn.

**student goals:**   The student's objectives for his or her participation in learning. Although much of what happens in a classroom is initiated by the teacher, students are capable of setting learning goals for themselves. For example, a student may strive to score 100 percent on the weekly spelling quiz, complete the chapter book on his or her own before the class deadline, or ignore assigned homework questions. Recognizing and encouraging students to set goals for themselves is a feature of a student-centered classroom.

**summative evaluation:** Occurs upon completion of a learning task. As the label suggests, there is a "summing up" of the task, usually in the form of a final grade for the project the student has completed. Summative evaluation can be combined with formative evaluation. For example, in a writing workshop environment, a teacher can provide formative evaluation for the duration of the workshop, guiding students toward growth and improvement, but eventually, the writing product will be submitted for the summative evaluation. From the learner's point of view, summative evaluation, particularly when the outcome is not favorable, may seem drastic and irrevocable. However, if the teacher has conferenced (providing formative evaluation) with students throughout the process of whatever project is underway, summative evaluation is likely to seem less teacher-oriented or arbitrary. Mandated local, state, and national assessments are summative, offering information about student performance in particular areas at a fixed point in the learning/teaching period.

**teaching goals:** Instructional objectives intended to fulfill classroom, campus, district, state, or national curricular expectations. Teaching goals do not have to counter student goals. For example, a teacher who wants all her third-grade students to be reading at the grade 3.0 level by the end of the first semester can set up minor goals and devise teaching activities that move the learners toward the teaching goal.

**technology applications:** The integration of computer technology and other media into language arts. This broad aspect of teaching includes, but is not limited to, the following types of teaching activities: integrating word processing into the writing process; using word processing tools to revise and edit drafts; using computer technology to produce writing and other types of texts; using the Internet as a research tool; producing a Web site that integrates elements of design and content; using desktop publishing programs to produce documents such as brochures, newspapers, flyers, and posters that support language arts topics under study; using multimedia equipment and/or software to produce language arts projects; or using computer technology and other multimedia technology to enhance teaching. Increasingly, teachers in all disciplines are expected to be adept at using technology and at facilitating students' use of technology. Technology applications are no longer the realm of experts; essentially, all teachers are expected to demonstrate some degree of expertise in this rapidly growing field.

# A New Look at Sample Items in TExES Preparation Manuals

The sample items in each TExES Preparation Manual are keyed to specific language arts competencies, so you will not find sample items that illustrate the terms and concepts we are discussing in this chapter. However, this does not mean that the terms do not occur in the sample items. Go back through the sample items in your TExES Preparation Manual, taking note of how many items include technology applications, reference to family support, learning difficulties, or English Language Learners. You might want to mark sections of those items in violet, our color code for this segment of our ELA TExES preparation. With the overview provided in this chapter, you should be able to use your knowledge of these pedagogical concerns to more easily identify the correct response in items qualified by these terms.

---

REFLECTION FOR YOUR TExES JOURNAL:    With this chapter, you are at the end of the "formal" study for your TExES exam provided in this book. Having worked through all the areas of language arts and through the integrated pedagogical practices discussed in this chapter, how do you assess your level of preparedness for your exam? What do you plan to do to increase your chances for success on the exam?

---

## Chapter Summary

- Your TExES preparation must include knowledge of teaching concerns that are integrated into all teaching disciplines: assessment, diversity, and technology.
- Read some of the Selected Resources to ensure you understand how these teaching concerns impact the teaching of English language arts.

## Selected Resources

Burke, J. (2003). *The English teacher's companion: A complete guide to classroom, curriculum, and the profession* (2nd ed.). Portsmouth, NH: Heinemann.
  Burke's Chapter 16, Success for All: Teaching Students with Special Needs, includes sections on English Language Learners and students with learning difficulties. The sections are short, but they offer sufficient information for the TExES candidate who needs to understand what these terms refer to. Chapter 26, The Politics of Education: Parents, School Boards, Politicians, and the Media, includes a few guidelines for maintaining contact with parents in order to foster growth in students' literacy skills.

Carger, C. L. (2004). Art and literacy with bilingual children. *Language Arts, 81*(4), 283-292.
  Carger describes a literacy learning research project that began when a group of Mexican American third graders saw similarities between the illustrations in the book they were reading and Van Gogh's paintings. (A previous teacher had read a book about Van Gogh to the children, and they became fascinated not only with his painting style but with his sad life as well.) The children, according to Carger, felt the illustrations were reminiscent of Van Gogh's brushstrokes. Carger's research involved using art as the core of literature discussions in this third-grade setting. She concludes that for English Language Learners who do not come from literacy-rich backgrounds, art may be a vehicle for fostering genuine engagement with literary texts. Carger's article is a good example of the adjustments that language arts teachers can make to meet the needs of ELL students. TExES candidates will find in this article numerous references to and applications of terms that occur in TEKS and educator standards.

Cronin, M. K. (2003). Rejecting senseless things: Promoting differentiation. *English Journal, 92*(4), 47-53.
  Cronin begins by pointing out that recognizing differences among students is the key to creating a student-centered rather than teacher-centered classroom. She describes several activities that are constructed to allow students to respond in ways that reflect their preferred learning styles. (Cronin analyzes her student responses using the terms Smagorinsky defines in the article included in this Selected Resources list.) Cronin's article includes many, many terms and explanations relevant to diversity, student-centered teaching, and assessment—the topics of this chapter.

Dong, Y. R. (2004). Don't keep them in the dark! Teaching metaphors to English language learners. *English Journal, 93*(4), 29-35.

> Dong points out that despite the prevalence of metaphorical ways of talking in day-to-day English, little is done in traditional second language instruction to teach ELL students how to unravel metaphor. Particularly illustrative is Dong's set of ten sentences, each of which uses the word *bread* in a distinct, metaphorical way. Numerous examples from actual classroom situations demonstrate how ELL students can be guided toward figuring out the meaning of English metaphorical language. This highly informative article is applicable to all levels of TExES preparation.

Eagleton, M., Guinee, K., & Langlais, K. (2003). Teaching Internet literacy strategies: The hero inquiry project. *Voices from the Middle, 10*(3), 28-35.

> The authors describe a research project for middle schoolers in which students are charged with researching a hero using Internet searches. TExES candidates will find the authors' description of how they taught students to conduct productive searches highly instructive and relevant to test preparation. The article includes examples of student responses to some of the research activities, a rubric designed to help students set their own goals for the project and assume responsibility for their grade, and descriptions of some of the final presentations.

Labbo, L. D., & others. (2003). Teacher wisdom stories: Cautions and recommendations for using computer-related technologies for literacy instruction. *The Reading Teacher, 52*(3). 300-304.

> This article is set up somewhat like Frequently Asked Questions about incorporating technology in literacy instruction. The TExES candidate will find many terms and explanations that are useful in understanding what constitutes technology applications in the classroom. In addition, numerous Web site addresses for technology-related information are included in the article.

Long, K. M. (2002). What every beginning teacher needs to know in technology. *English in Texas, 32*(1), 20-21.

> This article is particularly instructive for a TExES candidate with limited understanding of technology. Long presents fifteen activities designed to force preservice teachers to become familiar with the types of technology they will be expected to use in their classrooms. The activities include a simple word processing exercise, creating a spreadsheet, finding Internet Web sites that deal with teaching grammar and language, constructing a simple Web page, and finding Web sites appropriate to teaching *Romeo and Juliet.* Any TExES candidate who is even mildly technophobic or technology-challenged should read this article and actually work through some of the activities.

Maxwell, R. J., & Meiser, M. J. (2005). *Teaching English in middle and secondary schools* (4th ed.). Upper Saddle River, NJ: Prentice Hall.

> This comprehensive ELA pedagogy text includes a chapter on assessment, Chapter 12, Evaluating English Language Arts, that discusses authentic assessment and describes assessment activities for writing, literature, and oral language. Maxwell and Meiser offer a surprisingly thorough discussion of assessment (for TExES preparation purposes) in this chapter, which includes numerous sample rubrics and discussion of the issues that make assessment controversial.

McGee, L. M., & Richgels, D. J. (2004). *Literacy's beginnings: Supporting young readers and writers* (4th ed.). Boston: Pearson Education.

> Chapter 11, Diverse Learners, addresses issues and topics relevant to diversity and English Language Learners. Chapter 12, Assessment, includes discussion, examples, terms, and illustrations of children's work that clearly explain how assessment is integrated into language arts instruction at the elementary level. The subheadings in this book make it possible for TExES candidates to zoom in on particular areas of interest if they do not have enough time to read the entire chapters.

Smagorinsky, P. (1995). Multiple intelligences in the English class: An overview. *English Journal, 84*(8), 19-26.

Smagorinsky begins by describing how much more engaged in learning students appear to be when they are producing nontraditional presentations, such as media productions or dramatic performances enhanced by spectacular special effects. He provides a brief overview of Howard Gardner's multiple intelligences framework (spatial, linguistic, logical/mathematical, musical, bodily/kinesthetic, interpersonal, and intrapersonal). Smagorinsky suggests that limiting our teaching to traditional reading and writing methods prevents students from exploring other means of making meaning and expressing responses to the texts we examine in language arts classes. His extended discussion of student activities illustrates how attention to multiple intelligences can enrich students' experiences with language arts. This article can help the TExES candidate understand the importance of recognizing diversity in learning styles and adapting classroom activities to meet the needs of all learners.

Wollman-Bonilla, J. E. (2003). Email as genre: A beginning writer learns the conventions. *Language Arts, 81*(2), 126-134.

Through a case study of a 6-year-old learner, the author explores the differences in the child's use of conventions in email communication and traditional note or letter writing. Wollman-Bonilla offers numerous insights into the application of technology (in this case email communication) in literacy instruction. One interesting observation is that the child in the study readily learned the "conventions" of email communication and as readily switched to conventions of written communication in writing notes and letters. Wollman-Bonilla also speculates that email may be a hybrid between oral communication and traditional writing. There are numerous TExES-relevant terms used and in many cases defined throughout this article. The numerous examples of the focal child's emails and traditional writing are also highly beneficial to the TExES candidate who may have limited familiarity with children's writing.

# CHAPTER

# 8 Tactics for TExES Study

This final chapter offers tactics for approaching your TExES study efficiently and effectively. Chapter 1, you should recall, offers ten Study Strategies related to the content of the test. In this final chapter, we will discuss additional tactics for coordinating your study time in the "home stretch" of your test preparation, in the final weeks before you enter your testing room. Here are the tactics:

1. Implement the study plan suggested in Study Strategy 10 in Chapter 1.
2. Use your TExES Journal as a study aid.
3. Form a TExES study group.
4. Work through each item in the sample test in your TExES preparation manual using the analytical approach illustrated in the Exercises area of each chapter and applying the response strategies described in Test Prep Tip 6 in Chapter 1.
5. Develop a sample unit that incorporates concepts and practices suggested by TEKS and educator standards.

## Implement Your Study Plan

Make studying for your TExES exam a priority! Keep in mind that aggressive, focused study need only occur for about six weeks prior to taking your exam, so you should be able to stick to the plan suggested in Study Strategy 10. You do not want to find yourself in the predicament of wishing, on the day before the exam, that you had maintained the study schedule you originally devised. And you certainly do not want to go into the exam knowing that you are deficient in some of the areas on which you will be tested.

It is difficult to gauge exactly how much study any one candidate needs, but if you read and study the chapters in this book, if you complete your TExES Journal entries, if you read a few of the resources in the Selected Resources sections of each chapter, and if you review materials from your teacher preparation courses, you will probably spend 5 to 10 hours per language arts area, and perhaps 5 to 10 additional hours on the material in Chapter 7 and in this final chapter for a possible total of 60 hours of study. Even assuming that you need the full 60 hours to prepare adequately, that still means you can distribute your study period easily over six weeks, varying your study time from 30 minutes when you are very busy to longer, multiple-hour study sessions when you have more time available or when you can work with a study group.

## Your TExES Journal

Each chapter has included suggestions for reflecting on your familiarity with areas, concepts, terms, and pedagogical practices relevant to TExES. While it would be easy to dismiss the TExES Journal as a superfluous study aid, it is my hope that you have in fact kept a journal to track your progress in studying. Writing theory and practice shows us that writing is a way of learning, and that is my justification for suggesting a TExES Journal. My own TExES Journal, as I mentioned in Chapter 1, is a dark green spiral notebook, flagged with colored tabs to indicate where my notes for each language arts area occur. I have written entries in it from the day I conceived the idea of this book. And, as I have worked with the publisher and developed my drafts, I have continued to return to my TExES Journal notes. I have books, files, TExES-related documents, early drafts, and computer disks scattered all over my home office, but my TExES Journal has provided stability and centrality to my work on this book.

Do not underestimate the "grounding" nature of your TExES Journal—use it to keep yourself engaged in your study for your certification exam. And use it to prepare for your study group sessions.

## Socialized Study: Forming a Study Group

Many students find that studying in groups for TExES is a highly strategic move. If possible, you should form a small group of study partners who are all anticipating the same exam date. While there is some specialized knowledge required in each of the ELA/reading certification areas, I have tried to show in the chapters on each area that the *general* knowledge is relatively consistent among certification levels. Thus, your study group can be a mixture of EC-4, 4-8, and 8-12 TExES candidates.

I also suggest that you try to get an English professor to join your group as often as he or she has time for. Professors truly enjoy working with students who are highly motivated—as are TExES candidates. That professor will be a valuable resource in providing more comprehensive explanations of terms and concepts included in this book or of terms that are not addressed here. If you feel a bit uncomfortable about "imposing" on a professor in this way, you should be aware that such activities can be listed under our "community service" in our annual evaluation documents. If including a professor in your study group proves to be unfeasible, you can rely on email to contact professors with questions about specific terms or concepts and about additional suggested readings.

When you work in study groups, you should use your TExES Journal to identify terms and concepts that you remain unsure about even after working through this book. Remember that this book is not a replacement for the thorough attention to language arts areas that should have been provided in your teacher preparation courses. Instead, the book is designed to connect coursework to the TExES framework, and if this book represents your first exposure to TEKS, educator standards, and the TExES Preparation Manuals, some confusion about pedagogy, definitions of language arts terms, and about what might be on the test is likely to occur. The collaborative nature of a study group should do much to help you manage the confusion and anxiety that might occur as you prepare for your TExES exam.

What should you do in your study groups? Here are some suggestions:

- Quiz each other on fundamental terms and concepts in each language arts area. It might be a good idea to resort to the old-fashioned strategy of making up flash cards for terms that are particularly difficult for you to remember.
- Assign each other readings from the Suggested Resources lists. You may want to read more articles and chapters than you have time for, so split the work: Have each group member read one Suggested Resource for each chapter and report on it at your study group sessions.
- Work together to analyze the sample test items in your TExES Preparation Manual. If your group is made up of multiple certification level candidates, work through all the levels of sample items. Remember that the terms and concepts defined in this book for the most part apply to all levels of certification, so, for example, if you are testing at the 8-12 level, your knowledge should be broad enough to get you through the EC-4 and 4-8 items as well and vice versa. Keep in mind that the point of working through the sample items is to test your ability to analyze the items using the strategies presented in Test Prep Tip 6 and in the Exercises section of each chapter.

## Studying the TExES Sample Items

If you have read this book, studied the designated TExES-related documents, kept a TExES Journal, and developed a study plan, you should be able to attempt the sample items in your TExES Preparation Manual with a degree of confidence that you may not have felt when you began reading this book. If you have not already taken the sample test in your booklet, you should plan to work through the whole thing prior to your TExES test date. You should have some idea of how long it will take you to read the items carefully, to analyze the stem, and to use the principles presented in the book to eliminate the wrong responses. You should use the answer key in the preparation manual only after you have thoroughly analyzed each item; in other words, don't peek at the answer until you have actually studied the item and tried hard to implement the response strategies suggested in Test Prep Tip 6.

You should try out the sample test on your own, but eventually, you should include the sample items in your study group discussions. Working with your study partners to figure out the correct responses to the sample items will allow you to listen to others' rationales and understanding of the response strategies, and this socialization is likely to help you and your group members become better test takers.

## Devising Sample Units

At some point prior to taking your TExES exam, you should take some time to devise a sample teaching unit that incorporates various language arts principles into a variety of activities appropriate for your testing level and that connects each activity to TEKS and educator standards. Putting together a unit will provide an opportunity for you to think like a test-writing specialist since you will have to provide rationales for the activities, and those rationales will be based on the terms, concepts, and teaching principles over which you will be tested. As a test candidate, writing a unit will help you correlate TEKS expectations, educator standards, ELA content, and good teaching practices. This will be good preparation for figuring out correct responses to objective items on the actual test. When you look at the test items, you will know how to process each item from the perspective of the specialists who devised the test rather than from the perspective of an anxious test taker, and that point of view is likely to increase your chances of identifying the correct response on actual TExES exam questions.

As you work on your units, keep in mind that these are not the same types of units you would prepare for a teaching methods class or that you would present as lesson plans in an actual teaching situation. Writing units for classes or actual teaching entails a different type of thinking: In those cases, you have to incorporate what you are learning in class or what your academic supervisor requires. These TExES study strategy units are designed to prepare you for the test in two ways: (1) to focus your thinking on activities that pointedly reflect the ELA/Reading concepts that will show up on your exam and (2) to compel you to read through TEKS with an eye to correlating TEKS statements with your proposed activities. So, do not skip this preparation strategy simply because you have written teaching units in your education classes. The units in education classes are aimed at applications of general pedagogy. Devising a language arts unit, on the other hand, requires that you focus on the content of language arts: reading, writing, literature, oral language, and media literacy. Preparing the units in this chapter will help you anticipate how specific concepts, terms, and principles from the various language arts areas, TEKS, and educator standards may be presented in the teaching scenarios of the test items. Finally, you need to think about teaching activities in the context of what they are designed to teach students rather than how much fun they might be in the classroom. The activities you propose should be interesting for students, but they should clearly reflect the ELA and TEKS content you must know to pass the TExES exam.

The point of this TExES study tactic is not to determine whether you are filling in the chart "correctly" (as would be the case if you were preparing the unit for a class). Instead, you are envisioning a hypothetical teaching situation, which should enable you to view the teaching scenario items on your TExES exam from multiple perspectives: To fill in the chart, you need to think about the unit activities in terms of particular ELA areas; you need to rationalize about how the activity will promote the learners' competence in ELA; you need to connect the activity to TEKS. Keep in mind the creativity demonstrated by the activities described in the articles listed as resources. The activities you propose in the chart should demonstrate your understanding of best teaching practices and should indicate that you understand what each ELA area encompasses.

Finally, you might want to make these units a collaborative activity for your study group, instead of an independent study activity. Since no one will be grading your units, you need some feedback on the appropriateness of the activities and the soundness of the pedagogical principles, teaching goals, and TEKS connections you fill in for each activity.

## Sample Unit

Scenario: You teach ninth-grade language arts (English I in TEKS categories). You are teaching Sandra Cisneros' *The House on Mango Street* (1984), a short novel in which the narrator, a young Latina named Esperanza, tells us stories about important events that occurred in her neighborhood in Chicago. The novel ends with Esperanza ruminating about how she will leave her neighborhood one day, knowing, however, that she is likely to come back some day. It could be read as a story about the importance of place in shaping a young person's dreams and goals (see Figure 8.1).

## Application: EC-4 Unit

Scenario: You are a teacher of second graders. This suggests that you are in a largely self-contained classroom and you are responsible for teaching all subjects, except the highly specialized ones like fine arts and kinesiology. Devise a language arts unit structured around a science topic, such as studying the lives of ants. Assume that you have a science textbook that includes a chapter on this topic, that you have an ant farm in your classroom, and that you have numerous books and videos available in your school or classroom library in which ants are characters. For your test preparation unit, fill in the chart shown in Figure 8.2.

## Application: 4-8 Unit

Scenario: You are a sixth-grade language arts teacher at a middle school where the principal has recently mandated that all teachers should incorporate a unit on

**FIGURE 8.1**   Sample Unit on *The House on Mango Street*

| Type of Activity | Activity | Student Role | Teacher Goal(s) | ELA/Reading Skills Incorporated into the Activity | TEKS Addressed |
|---|---|---|---|---|---|
| Preparation/ introduction | Prereading activity: Students are to bring a picture set in a house in which they have lived and about which they have good memories. In class, students will write a short reflective piece on a significant event that occurred in that house. Pictures students bring will be displayed on a bulletin board labeled "Our Houses." Students will orally share their memories with their classmates. | As they share their memories with their classmates, students will tack their house/place pictures onto the bulletin board.<br><br>Students will begin to form generalizations about how places and homes influence us. | To introduce students to an important thematic element of the novel (the impact of home and neighborhood on a young person's life).<br><br>To prepare students for the vignette-type chapters of the novel.<br><br>To help students recognize similarities between their own memories of important places and the recollections presented by the Hispanic narrator of the novel. | Prereading<br>Socialization<br>Collaborative work<br>Short writing<br>Oral language<br>Multiculturalism | English I Reading/literary concepts TEKS that relate to understanding the theme of a literary text.<br><br>English I Reading/culture TEKS that address finding connections between the students' own culture and that presented in literary texts. |
| Reading | Literature response journals | Students write several entries in their literature response journals each night. They share their responses orally in class at the beginning of each day's discussion of the novel. | To help students become engaged with the story.<br><br>To prepare students to participate actively in class discussion about the novel. | Active reading<br>Journal writing<br>Critical reading<br>Oral language | English I Reading/literary response TEKS that address the construction of response to literary texts.<br><br>English I Reading/comprehension TEKS that address using various reading strategies to find connections with texts. |
| Oral language | Dramatization of specific chapters: Working in groups, students write a script to dramatize the events in one chapter of the book. Each group has a different chapter. | Students write dialog and stage the scene in their chapter. | To help students visualize the events that Esperanza recounts in her "memoir" of her childhood.<br><br>To help students understand the narrative techniques Cisneros uses to tell her story. | Reader's theater<br>Oral language<br>Writing | English I Listening/speaking/audiences TEKS that address making dramatic presentations of literary texts. |

| Media literacy | Watching selected scenes from the movie, *The Shipping News* (1999), that focus on the importance of the house which the main character, Quoyle, moves into when he relocates to Newfoundland. The house has been in his family a very long time, but it has been moved from its original location and has been abandoned for decades. Quoyle moves in reluctantly—but because of its state of disrepair—but quickly realizes the importance of the house in shaping his family's identity. The movie includes many spectacular shots of the house which sits tethered by steel cables to a cliff overlooking the brutal Newfoundland waters. | After watching the selected scenes, students will react to the scenes and orally share their responses. Guided discussion from the teacher should help students see connections between the novel, the movie scenes, and their own experiences with homes, houses, and places. | To help students understand the theme of the novel by considering a similar theme in a visual text. | Whole class discussion<br>Media literacy<br>Socialization<br>Finding relevance in literature<br>Connecting film techniques to literary techniques | English I *Viewing/representing/analysis* TEKS that address contrasting messages conveyed by visual and print media. |
| Writing | Postreading/culminating activity: Students will write a chapter in the style of the chapters in the book. This added chapter, tentatively titled "Back on Mango Street," will be set five years after the closing chapter of the book. | After writing their chapters, students will read them orally to classmates. | To provide an opportunity for students to think critically about the outcome of the novel.<br><br>To use writing as a means of exploring the issues raised by the novel. | Critical thinking<br>Creative writing<br>Oral language | English I TEKS in *Writing/purposes* that address writing in a style appropriate to the assigned task and audience. |

127

FIGURE 8.2    EC-4 Practice Unit: *Exploring the Lives of Ants*

| Type of Activity | Activity | Student Role | Teacher Goal(s) | ELA/Reading Skills Incorporated into the Activity | TEKS Addressed |
|---|---|---|---|---|---|
| Preparation/ introduction | | | | | |
| Reading | | | | | |
| Oral language | | | | | |
| Media literacy | | | | | |
| Writing | | | | | |

FIGURE 8.3   4-8 Practice Unit: *Patriotism*

| Type of Activity | Activity | Student Role | Teacher Goal(s) | ELA/Reading Skills Incorporated into the Activity | TEKS Addressed |
|---|---|---|---|---|---|
| Preparation/ introduction | | | | | |
| Reading | | | | | |
| Oral language | | | | | |
| Media literacy | | | | | |
| Writing | | | | | |

FIGURE 8.4    8-12 Practice Unit: *Lord of the Flies*

| Type of Activity | Activity | Student Role | Teacher Goal(s) | ELA/Reading Skills Incorporated into the Activity | TEKS Addressed |
|---|---|---|---|---|---|
| Preparation/ introduction | | | | | |
| Reading | | | | | |
| Oral language | | | | | |
| Media literacy | | | | | |
| Writing | | | | | |

patriotism into the curriculum. The principal has explained at a faculty meeting that the rationale for this requirement is development of citizenship in the school's children and helping students relate school activities to national and international events. However, the principal reminds you that the focus of your activities should be to develop language arts skills your students need in order to succeed in higher grades and to function effectively in real-world situations. Assume that you have a school and classroom library that includes classroom sets of many young adult novels. Also assume that you have in your classroom a television and VCR and/or DVD player as well as five state-of-the-art computers with total access to the Internet. Fill in the chart in Figure 8.3 with the activities and rationales you would propose for this unit.

As you fill in this chart, you should keep in mind that most textbooks about teaching ELA strongly advocate using thematic units. Although the principal has mandated the theme, in this scenario you should acknowledge that it is a theme that can be managed through diverse, student-centered, pedagogically sound activities.

## Application: 8-12 Unit

Scenario: You are about to launch a unit on *Lord of the Flies* (1959), a required novel in your school's English II (sophomore) curriculum. Keep in mind that in an actual classroom situation, you would have multiple activities for each language arts area. For this test preparation activity, however, you simply want to practice devising activities that show you understand the basic elements of each ELA area designated in the chart, so only one activity is sufficient for each language arts area. Also remember that when you teach a literary text, you should work at helping students appreciate the text and its literary qualities; in other words, you should be fostering their love of literature. Use the unit chart in Figure 8.4 to devise some activities that you could use in teaching *Lord of the Flies*.

# AFTERWORD

## A Note from the Author

When your TExES exam is over, when you have your passing scores in hand, when you have applied for your teaching certificate, when you look forward to being in charge of your own classroom, you will still have a long way to go as an ELA teacher. Leila Christenbury's (2000) comparison of teaching to a journey nicely prepares us for what we have ahead of us as we enter careers in teaching:

> Regardless of how prepared or . . . unprepared for English teaching you may be, you are from day one a teacher making a journey. But the paradox is that from day one you will continue to become, evolve, and change as a teacher. It is, oddly enough, happily enough, a simultaneous process of both being a teacher and becoming a teacher. The two events are not separate and actually are not mutually exclusive. (p. 4)

Christenbury's comment reminds us that there is much more to being a teacher of ELA than simply taking proscribed English and education courses—or passing a teacher certification exam. Clearly, such requirements are a vital part of teacher preparation, but teaching is a learning process that will continue as long as you are a teacher.

Although passing your certification exam may seem to be an obstacle in your teaching journey, it is actually more of a gateway. Once you are fully credentialed as an ELA educator, you will have a "license" to practice and apply the theories and strategies you are expected to know for your TExES exams. Preparing for your required certification exam should not get in the way of your excitement over preparing to enter a career in teaching.

Let me remind you my approach has been pragmatic: My goal is to help you pass your TExES exam. The philosophy, the attitudes, the beliefs you need to take with you into your ELA classrooms are the domain of your education classes. Your teaching education should have occurred in your college classrooms where you should have practiced the strategies that work in classrooms, where you should have mastered the content of ELA, where you should have debated issues that are important to teachers.

It is my hope that this book has allowed you to make connections between your teacher preparation courses and the Texas Education Agency's and the State Board for Educator Certification's expectations for new teachers. Understanding those connections is a vital part of succeeding on your TExES exam. TExES is only one of the many milestones you must reach and pass on your teaching journey—but it is a significant milestone, one that could cause you to trip on your journey toward professionalism or one that you could leap over easily if you are adequately prepared. This book is designed to help you do the latter—to leap rather than stumble—as you meet the challenge of your certification exam.

# REFERENCES

Anaya, R. A. (1972). *Bless me, Ultima.* Berkeley, CA: Tonatiuh International.

Avi. (1991). *Nothing but the truth.* New York: Avon Books.

Burke, J. (2003). *The English teacher's companion* (2nd ed.). Portsmouth, NH: Heinemann.

Christenbury, L. (2000). *Making the journey: Being and becoming a teacher of English language arts* (2nd ed.). Portsmouth, NH: Heinemann.

Cisneros, S. (1984). *The house on Mango Street.* New York: Vintage Books.

Columbus, C. (Director). (2001/2002). *Harry Potter and the Sorcerer's Stone* [motion picture, DVD]. United States: Warner Home Video.

Creech, S. (1994). *Walk two moons.* New York: Scholastic.

DePaola, T. (1983). *The legend of the bluebonnet.* New York: G. P. Putnam's Sons.

Golding, W. (1959/1999). *Lord of the flies.* Penguin Great Books of the 20th Century Series. New York: Penguin Group.

Goulden, N. R. (1998). Implementing speaking and listening standards: Information for English teachers. *English Journal 88*(1), 90-96.

Hallstrom, L. (Director). (1999). *The shipping news* [motion picture, DVD]. United States: Walt Disney Video.

Krueger, E. (1998). Media literacy does work, trust me. *English Journal 87*(1), 17-20.

Maxwell, R. J., & Meiser, M. J. (2005). *Teaching English in middle and secondary schools* (4th ed.) Upper Saddle River, NJ: Prentice-Hall.

Poe, E. A. (2004). The cask of amontillado. In L. Kirszner & S. Mandell (Eds.), *Literature: Reading, reacting, writing* (5th ed.; pp. 243-249). Boston: Heinle. (Original publication date 1846.)

Rowling, J. K. (1997). *Harry Potter and the sorcerer's stone.* New York: Scholastic Press.

Scieszka, J. (1989). *The true story of the three little pigs.* New York: Scholastic Press.

Shyamalan, M. N. (Director). (1999). The *sixth sense* [motion picture, VHS]. United States: Hollywood Pictures and SpyGlass Entertainment.

Silvey, A. (2004). *100 best books for children.* Boston: Houghton Mifflin.

State Board for Educator Certification. (2002a). *English Language Arts and Reading (Grades 4-8) Standards.* Retrieved August 22, 2004 from http://www.sbec.state.tx.us/SBECOnline/standtest/standards/4-8elar.pdf

State Board for Educator Certification. (2002b). *English Language Arts and Reading (Grades 8-12) Standards.* Retrieved August 22, 2004 from http://www.sbec.state.tx.us/SBECOnline/standtest/standards/8-12elar.pdf

State Board for Educator Certification. (2002c). *English Language Arts and Reading (Early Childhood-Grade 4) Standards.* Retrieved August 22, 2004 from http://www.sbec.state.tx.us/SBECOnline/standtest/standards/ec4elar.pdf

State Board for Educator Certification. (2003a). *Texas Examinations of Educator Standards Preparation Manual 131 English Language Arts and Reading 8-12.* Retrieved August 22, 2004 from http://www.texes.nesinc.com/prepmanuals/PDFs/TExES_fld131_prepmanu

State Board for Educator Certification. (2003b). *Texas Examinations of Educator Standards Preparation Manual 117 English Language Arts and Reading 4-8.* Retrieved August 22, 2004 from http://www.texes.nesinc.com/prepmanuals/PDFs/TExES_fld117_prepmanu

State Board for Educator Certification. (2003c). *Texas Examinations of Educator Standards Preparation Manual 101 Generalist EC-4*. Retrieved August 21, 2004 from http://www.excet.nesinc.com/prepmanuals/PDFs/TExES_fld101_prepmanual.pdf

State Board for Educator Certification. (2003d). *Texas Examinations of Educator Standards Preparation Manual 103 Bilingual Generalist EC-4*. Retrieved July 8, 2004 from http://www.excet.nesinc.com/prepmanuals/PDFs/TExES_fld103_prepmanual.pdf

State Board for Educator Certification. (2003e). *Texas Examinations of Educator Standards Preparation Manual 104 English as a Second Language(ESL) / Generalist EC-4*. Retrieved July 8, 2004 from http://www.excet.nesinc.com/prepmanuals/PDFs/TExES_fld104_prepmanual.pdf

State Board for Educator Certification. (2003f). *Texas Examinations of Educator Standards Preparation Manual 111 Generalist 4-8*. Retrieved July 8, 2004 from http://www.excet.nesinc.com/prepmanuals/PDFs/TExES_fld111_prepmanual.pdf

State Board for Educator Certification. (2003g). *Texas Examinations of Educator Standards Preparation Manual 119 Bilingual Generalist 4-8*. Retrieved August 22, 2004 from http://www.excet.nesinc.com/prepmanuals/PDFs/TExES_fld119_prepmanual.pdf

State Board for Educator Certification. (2003h). *Texas Examinations of Educator Standards Preparation Manual 113 Generalist 4-8*. Retrieved August 22, 2004 from http://www.excet.nesinc.com/prepmanuals/PDFs/TExES_fld113_prepmanual.pdf

State Board for Educator Certification. (2003i). *Texas Examinations of Educator Standards Preparation Manual 120 English as a Second Language (ESL)/Generalist 4-8*. Retrieved February 27, 2005 from http://www.texes.nesinc.com/prepmanuals/PDFs/TExES_fld120_prepmanual.pdf

State Board for Educator Certification. (2004). *Approved educator standards*. Retrieved July 17, 2004 from http://www.sbec.state.tx.us/SBECOnline/standtest/edstancertfieldlevl.asp

Texas Education Agency. (1998a). Texas Administrative Code (TAC), Title 19, Part II Chapter 10. Texas Essential Knowledge and Skills for English Language Arts and Reading. Subchapter A. Elementary. Retrieved August 22, 2004 from http://www.tea.state.tx.us/rules/tac/chapter110/ch110a.html

Texas Education Agency. (1998b). Texas Administrative Code (TAC), Title 19, Part II Chapter 10. Texas Essential Knowledge and Skills for English Language Arts and Reading. Subchapter B. Middle School. Retrieved August 22, 2004 from http://www.tea.state.tx.us/rules/tac/chapter110/ch110b.html

Texas Education Agency. (1998c). Texas Administrative Code (TAC), Title 19, Part II Chapter 10. Texas Essential Knowledge and Skills for English Language Arts and Reading. Subchapter C. High School. Retrieved August 22, 2004 from http://www.tea.state.tx.us/rules/tac/chapter110/ch110c.html

Welles, O. (Director). (2001). *Citizen Kane* [motion picture, DVD]. United States: Turner Home Entertainment. (Original release date 1941.)

# INDEX

Bilingual exams, vii, 1, 4, 8
Burke, J., 97

Calderonello, A., Martin, V. S.,
    & Blair, K. L., 53
Certification candidate
    categories, vi
Certification levels, 1
Christenbury, L., 86, 129
Connections, TEKS, educator
    standards, test competen-
    cies, 2, 9

Definitions, English Language
    Arts terms
    literature, 64–68
    media literacy, 101–104
    oral language, 86–90
    reading, 23, 26–31
    writing, 41, 43–50
Definitions, general pedagogy
    terms
    annotated list of resources for
        further study, 118–120
    assessment, 114, 116, 117
    collaborative learning, 114
    culture, 1, 65, 115
    diversity, 1, 113, 115
    English Language Learners,
        113, 115, 117
    ethnicity and classroom
        practice, 115
    learning difficulties, 113, 116,
        117
    parental involvement, 113,
        115, 117
    student-centered, 116
    technology, 113, 117

Educator standards
    as a study aid, 8
    connection to TEKS, 6
    definition, 8
    relevance to TExES, 8
    Web site, 8

English as a Second Language
    exams (ESL), vii, 1, 4, 8
English courses and TExES, 3–4,
    9–10
English Language Arts
    annotated list of resources for
        further study, 16–17
    ELA areas, 4
    test content, 1, 9
    tests that include ELA
        content, vi

Generalist exams, 1, 4, 8
Goulden, N. R., 83

Hult, C. A., & Huckin, T. H., 53

Krueger, E., 99–100

Literature
    4-8 literature content, 62
    annotated list of resources for
        further study, 79–82
    classroom practices, 68–69
    definitions of basic terms,
        64–68
    EC-4 literature content, 62
    familiarity with K–12
        literature, 72–73
    literature content test items,
        73–75
    overview, 61–62
    practice test items, 69–72
    sample 8-12 essay, 78
    study chart, 63
    study materials, 64
    the TExES 8-12 essay, 75–77
    TExES journal prompts, 62,
        64, 69, 79
    working definition, 61
Long, K. M., 99

Maxwell, R. J., & Meiser, M. J.,
    88

Media literacy
    annotated list of resources for
        further study, 109–112
    definitions of basic terms,
        101–104
    EC-4, 98
    introduction, 97
    nonprint texts, examples, 98
    overview, 98–100
    practice test items, 105–108
    study chart, 101
    study strategies, 108–109
    teaching practices and
        attitudes, 104–105
    TExES journal prompts, 100,
        105, 109
    working definition, 98

National Council of Teachers of
    English (NCTE), 15

Oral language
    annotated list of resources for
        further study, 95–96
    classroom practices, 90–91
    definitions of basic terms,
        86–90
    overview, 83–84
    practice test items, 91–94
    study chart, 85
    study materials, 84–85
    TExES journal prompts, 84,
        86, 91, 95
    working definition, 83

Practice test questions
    See TExES EC-4, TExES 4-8,
        TExES 8-12

Reading
    annotated list of resources for
        further study, 37–38
    classroom practices, 31
    definitions of basic terms, 23,
        26–31

Reading (*continued*)
    overview, 21–22
    practice test items, 33–36
    reading instruction, 21
    reading materials for K–12
        students, 32
    study chart, 23–24
    study materials, 22
    TExES journal prompts, 22,
        31, 36
    working definition, 21
Resources for further study
    comprehensive, 16–17
    reading, 37–38
    literature, 79–82
    writing, 58–60
    oral language, 95–96
    media literacy, 109–112
    general pedagogy, 118–120

Sample tests
    *See* TExES preparation
        manuals
State Board for Educator
        Certification (SBEC)
    educator standards, 2
    in TExES framework, 2
    Web site, 1
Study plan, 19–20, 121–122
Study strategies, 5, 8, 9, 10–13,
        13–14, 14–15, 15–16, 17–19
    consulting suggested
        resources, 15
    media literacy, 108–109
    organizing study materials,
        14–15, 22–25, 41, 63–64,
        84–85, 100
    sample units, 124–129
    study groups, 122–123

Teaching practices and attitudes
    literature, 68–69
    media literacy, 104
    oral language, 90–91
    reading, 31
    writing, 40–41, 50–51
Test competencies, 9
Test items
    response strategies (Test Prep
        Tip 6), 12

sample tests in preparation
    manuals, 13, 36, 58, 77, 94,
    109
structure, 10–13
types, 11, 73–75
Test Prep Tips, 1, 2, 4, 7, 9, 12,
    20, 32, 54, 73, 76
Texas Essential Knowledge and
    Skills (TEKS)
    applicable grade levels for
        ELA exams, 5–6
    as a study aid, 5–7
    assessment, 113–114
    categories, 6
    definition, 5
    key ELA terms embedded in
        TEKS, 6–7
    research process, 51–52
    technology, 113–114
    Web site, 5
Texas Examination of Educator
    Standards (TExES)
    bilingual, 4, 8
    certification levels, 1
    English Language Arts and
        Reading, vi
    ESL, 4, 8
    generalist exams, 1
    relationship among TEKS,
        educator standards, and
        test competencies, 2–3,
        13–14, 22, 41, 62, 84,
        100–101
    test content, 1
    tests with ELA components,
        vi
TExES 4-8
    note for 4-8 candidates, 62
    practice test items, 34–35,
        55–56, 70–71, 92–93,
        106–107
TExES 8-12
    essay, 75–77
    practice test items, 35–36,
        56–57, 71–72, 75, 93–94,
        107–108
    sample essay, 78
TExES EC-4
    ELA content, 1
    note for EC-4 test candidates,
        4, 8, 62–63, 98

practice test items, 33–34,
    54–55, 69–70, 91–92,
    105–106
TExES essay
    *See* TExES 8-12; Literature
TExES journal
    as study aid, 17–19, 122
    journal entry prompts, 20, 22,
        23, 31, 36, 39, 41, 58, 62, 64,
        69, 79, 84, 86, 91, 95, 100,
        105, 109, 114, 118
    sample, 18
TExES preparation manuals, 1–2
    language arts areas, 4
    responding to sample test
        items, 10, 36, 58, 77, 94, 117
    rubric for 8-12 essay, 76
    sample tests as a study aid,
        123–124,
    sample tests, 3
    test competencies, 9
    test information included in
        manuals, 2
*The Sixth Sense*, 97

Weaver, C., 53
Writing
    annotated list of resources for
        further study, 58–60
    definitions of basic terms, 41,
        43–50
    familiarity with K–12 student
        writing, 53–54
    grammar knowledge, 52–53
    linguistics, 53
    practice test items, 54–57
    reflecting about one's writing
        process, 39
    research process in TEKS,
        51–52
    study chart, 42
    TExES journal prompts, 39,
        49, 58
    teaching practices, 40, 50–51
    working definition, 40

Zemelman, S., & Daniels, H., 51